New Forest

Gerald Ponting

About the author

Gerald Ponting is a keen photographer and is well-known as a speaker at many local societies. Working with colleagues, he has written 22 books and booklets concerning the history of several Hampshire communities. Gerald was brought up in a village on the edge of the New Forest. He spent ten years of his life in the Outer Hebrides. In 1978 he was presented with a British Archaeological Award for studies of the Standing Stones of Callanish, Isle of Lewis.

He was a Biology teacher for 30 years, taking early retirement in 1992, after which he spent some years working as a Blue Badge Tourist Guide for Hampshire, Wiltshire and Dorset.

D0293421

Landmark Publishing

At each road entrance to the New Forest National Park, there stands an elegant hand-carved wooden pillar bearing the Park logo

NEW FOREST NATIONAL PARK

Great spotted woodpecker

Dedication

To the memory of my parents, Ernest and Nellie Ponting, who loved the Forest in all its moods.

Acknowledgements

The author wishes to thank the following for information, advice and proof-reading (1st edition) – Peter Bennett, Barbara Burbridge, Bridget Hall (Forestry Commission), Barbara Hillier, Anthony Light, Philippa Newnham, Sara St George (New Forest District Council Leisure Services) and Sue Westwood (Verderers' clerk); also the staff of many of the attractions detailed; and fellow members of Viewfinders of Romsey Camera Club for the loan of photographs.

Landmark Publishing thanks Michael Bell of Bells Bookshop, Halifax, Yorkshire ☎ (01422) 365468 for supplying the material upon which the maps in this book are based.

The New Forest

Contents

(The) 'intermixture of wood and pasturage, with large separations of heath, give a variety to the forest, which a boundless continuance of woody scenery could not exhibit.'

*Remarks on Forest Scenery by William Gilpin
(Vicar of Boldre), 1791*

Top Tips

Visit the **New Forest Centre in Lyndhurst** for a fascinating insight into the history and traditions of the Forest.

The **hop-on-hop-off open-top buses** of the New Forest Tour provide an easy way to discover the area without using the car.

Explore the depths of the ancient woodlands - set out on foot, rent a bicycle, hire a pony, use a good map, follow a waymarked trail - and get away from the crowds.

Rhinefield and Bolderwood Ornamental Drives are at their best in early November, with ancient beech trees displaying spectacular autumn colours.

Visit the viewing platform at **Bolderwood Deer Sanctuary** to see fallow deer – the easy way to have more than a glimpse of the Forest's elusive inhabitants.

Take a quiet stroll across the open heathland to see ponies and cattle grazing, to watch and listen to birds, to enjoy the colours of gorse, heather and other wild flowers.

Spend a day at Beaulieu: Abbey, Palace House and National Motor Museum - ruins, gardens, rides, a stately home, historic cars - truly a day out for all the family.

Ponies are frequently seen grazing on heathland or on lawns but they are also free to graze in the unenclosed woodlands

For garden lovers, both **Exbury** and the smaller **Furzey Gardens** are wonderful in early summer.

Look out for special events during your visit – festivals, shows, carnivals, exhibitions, markets and so on.

Make sure you try some of the **delicious local produce** bearing the New Forest Marque, from venison to ice-cream and from eggs to honey.

Use the information in this guide to find places to go, things to do, that will suit all the family.

There is nowhere else quite like the New Forest. It is the biggest area of largely unspoilt countryside in the lowlands of southern Britain and one of the few medieval forests remaining in Europe. Against all the odds, an ancient landscape of majestic woodlands, gorse-covered heathland and boggy valleys has survived into the twenty-first century.

William the Conqueror set this area apart for the 'beasts of the forest'. Wild boar disappeared long ago but red, roe and fallow deer still live in the woods. Ponies and cattle belonging to the commoners also graze in the open Forest. They prevent the growth of scrub and have been called the 'architects of the Forest landscape'.

The right of pasture was first granted to the common people as compensation for the imposition of Forest Law. Harsh penalties were inflicted on anyone who harmed the deer or otherwise interfered with the King's pleasure in the hunt. The Crown still owns much of the Forest, managed today with nature conservation and amenity pre-cedence over timber production.

The woods and heaths, the small farms, villages and estates, the bogs, ponds and streams together form a complex mosaic of habitats, each one with its own distinctive wildlife. However, the whole is greater than the sum of its parts, making the New Forest an area of the greatest international importance biologically.

Today, the New Forest is many things to many people. To the commoners and foresters it is a way of life as well as a livelihood. To botanists, entomologists, bird-watchers and the like, it has one of the best range of habitats in Britain and must be carefully protected. For many commuters, it provides an opportunity

Leave the car & explore!

While this book is arranged in the conventional fashion of tours by road, it is hoped that many visitors will avoid over-use of the car. All touring motorists should leave the car behind as often as possible; that is the only way to really get to know the Forest. Arrive by rail or coach and most parts of the Forest can be explored by a combination of walking, cycling and public transport.

However, I have not seen it as the purpose of this book to give detailed instructions for individual walks or cycle rides. There are several other books and maps which fulfil this function admirably. Any one of them would prove a valuable supplement to this book. In addition, the OS Explorer map of the New Forest becomes essential if the visitor intends to penetrate into the heart of the woodlands. Here peace and tranquillity can always be found, even on summer weekends when the car parks are overflowing.

Caring for the forest

It is hoped that most visitors to the New Forest will be aware of and will observe the Country Code, summarised in the adage 'take nothing but photographs, leave nothing but footprints' (although even footprints can be damaging in some habitats!). The Forest, however, is a very special place so it has its own more extensive code of advice for visitors.

• Stay below 40mph (64kph) on unfenced roads

This greatly reduces the number of accidents affecting ponies, cattle and deer, especially at night. Take the greatest care when passing animals, as they do not understand cars and may make unpredictable movements.

• Use the New Forest car parks

There are around 120 of them, so there is no need to cause congestion and damage to verges by parking on the roadside. It is, of course, advisable to lock your car and not to leave valuable items in it.

• Admire the ponies and donkeys, but do not feed them

Animals soon associate cars and people with food. This attracts them to the roadside where they are in danger; some may become aggressive towards visitors when no snack is forthcoming! If a pony lays its ears back alongside its head, back away promptly – this is a threatening posture. Never come between a mare and her foal, as she will see this as a threat and react accordingly.

• You may walk on any track or footpath in the Forest

unless there is a notice telling you otherwise. Keeping to paths greatly reduces disturbance to wildlife habitats. On Ordnance Survey maps of the Forest, double dashed lines generally indicate a wide, often gravel, track; a single dashed line indicates any other track or footpath.

• Cycling is permitted on waymarked routes only

Cyclists must not use other tracks, paths or open heathland. Wheel-spins and skidding in particular cause erosion. Cyclists should give way to horse-riders and walkers.

• Fire is a real threat to Forest habitats and wildlife

The making of any kind of camp-fire is prohibited. Barbecue sites are provided at two car parks.

• Keep your dog under control at all times

Dogs can cause considerable trouble both for wildlife and for grazing animals. Dogs must be kept on a lead in inclosures.

• Litter is unsightly and can kill animals

Take it home with you or put it into the bins provided.

Forest Bye-laws

These are listed on panels at every car park. They include a prohibition on any picking or gathering of plant material. However, collecting fungi is permitted – for personal consumption only. Of course, no-one should consume wild fungi unless they are capable of positively distinguishing between palatable and poisonous species! Specific banning notices are displayed in some woods to help conserve the important fungi populations.

to live in the depths of the countryside while working in the surrounding urban areas.

While visitors are always welcome, there have to be some restrictions if the Forest is to survive the pressures caused by visitor numbers (*see* 'Caring for the Forest', p.9). Golfers, anglers, horse-riders, model-boat enthusiasts and many others are catered for, in one part of the Forest or another. Management of the Forest often involves resolving apparently conflicting interests.

New Forest Donkeys

Grey squirrel

Spider's web on an autumn morning

Docile bullocks enjoying sunshine on a winter afternoon

A newborn donkey foal having one of his first meals

The history of the New Forest

The area now occupied by the New Forest would have been relatively unattractive for settlement in prehistoric times; the soil is mostly poor, due to the sands, clay and gravels which make up the local geology. Around 3,000 years ago, though, Bronze Age people cleared woodland to grow crops. Their farming techniques resulted in soil deterioration, thus producing the extensive heathland. The tribes buried their dead in round barrows, of which around 200 are known in the Forest.

Iron Age people constructed a number of hillforts, of which the best preserved today is Buckland Rings at

Above: Sulphur tuft fungus on a decaying stump

Right: Just two of the 2700 species of fungi which grow in the Forest

Lymington. In Roman times in-digenous resources were used to produce a distinctive type of pottery. Local clay was fired in kilns using the ample supply of firewood. The resulting 'New Forest ware' was distributed throughout southern England.

Our knowledge of the Forest in the 'Dark Ages', the period between about 410AD and 1066, is sparse. However, most of the main settlements known in the Forest area today must have been established by the Saxon period – they are mentioned in Domesday Book and their place-names have Anglo-Saxon origins.

Creation of the Forest

It was around 1079 that William the Conqueror ordered the creation of a new hunting reserve in the area previously known as Ytene. The new name was first recorded in 1086 as Nova Foresta, 'New Forest', in Domesday Book. At that time, a 'forest' was an area of countryside, not necessarily woodland, set aside for the royal beasts of the chase. This provided both sport and meat for the king and his retinue.

The New Forest was considerably bigger then, its perambulation (or boundary) surrounding an area stretching from the Solent almost to Salisbury and from the Avon valley to Southampton Water. It has often been stated that William displaced whole communities to create the Forest, but in fact the area was very sparsely populated to begin with.

The Forest Law

The local inhabitants became subject to the harsh Forest Law, administered by the Verderers' Court. The penalties for poaching the king's deer were death or mutilation. Cutting vegetation which gave food and shelter for the deer was prohibited. No Forest land could be enclosed, so the local people were permitted to graze their ponies, cattle and pigs on the open land. However, the animals had to be taken back to the peasants' tiny holdings in winter, when the scant grazing was reserved for the deer, and also during the 'fence month'. This was the period around midsummer's day when most of the young deer were born.

In 1217, the 'Charter of the Forest' relaxed the Forest Law. The harsher penalties were abandoned and people were allowed, on suitable payment, to enlarge their holdings by fencing more land.

Timber for ships

Wood was, of course, a primary raw material in the Middle Ages. Gradually, the production of timber became more important than the protection of deer, resulting in the first-ever parliamentary Act on tree-protection being passed as early as 1483.

The earliest record of oak from the New Forest being used to build naval ships dates from 1611. A large warship required the timber from at least sixty trees, each around 200 years old. With the demand for vessels to protect England's coasts, it is hardly surprising that, in 1698, Parliament passed an 'Act for the Increase and Preservation of Timber in the New Forest'.

This instituted the 'rolling power of inclosure'. Up to 6,000 acres (2,430 hectares) of the Forest could be fenced at any one time, to grow timber for naval ship-building. Once young trees had grown too large to be affected by grazing animals, the fences could be removed and the woodland opened for grazing. Then another area up to the same acreage could be enclosed and planted. The Act also banned the practice of pollarding – the cutting of branches for animal feed.

Disputes between Crown & Commoners

The last king to use his right to hunt in the Forest was James II in the 1680s. Deer were soon seen as a hindrance to efficient timber production, as fences were no obstacle to them; they ate tree seedlings, thus preventing regeneration. Eventually, this led to the 'New Forest Deer Removal Act' of 1851. The plan to eliminate all the deer inevitably failed, but numbers fell considerably.

The Act contained other sweeping changes. The maximum area of 'rolling inclosure' was greatly increased. Within the first year, 4,000 acres (1,620 hect-

---

Commoners' Charter

Like that of 1698, the 1851 Act resulted in conflict between the Crown's interest in timber production and the commoners' interest in grazing. The problems were largely resolved by the New Forest Act of 1877, sometimes called the 'Commoners' Charter'. The Verderers' Court was re-established with a totally different role – to protect the rights of the commoners. The rolling power of inclosure was ended. The more ancient woods were to be left unenclosed, so that animals could graze in them.

---

ares) were planted, mostly with conifers. All commoners' rights had to be registered by a new committee – which systematically refused many applications and reduced the value of others. As a result, the number of commoners declined, as did the amount of grazing available to their animals.

Changes in the twentieth century

During and between World War I and II, many trees were felled and large areas were planted with conifers. In 1923, the Crown lands became the responsibility of the new Forestry Commission.

In the second half of the twentieth century measures were taken to improve conditions for visitors, while reducing their environmental impact; to put wildlife conservation much nearer the top of the 'Forest agenda'; and to reduce the risks of animals being killed or injured by traffic.

In the early 1960s, cattle grids were installed where roads crossed the Forest perambulation – previously, ponies had often strayed outside, sometimes raiding gardens! At around the same time the A31 trunk road was fenced to reduce accidents involving animals – soon followed by the fencing of the A35 and A337. All other roads through the New Forest remain unfenced, but with a blanket speed limit of 40mph (64kph) introduced in the 1990s.

In the 1960s and 1970s, the impact of visitors and their cars, tents and caravans was having a disastrous effect on the Forest. At that time, there was nothing to prevent motorists driving onto the open Forest and parking wherever their vehicles could take them. The answer was to provide many carefully-sited car parks, with ditches and barriers to make most of the Forest car-free. By 1976 this had been completed, along with the establishment of official camping sites.

Wildlife conservation

The Act passed in 1877 recognised the amenity value of the unfenced and grazed woodlands, giving them a grand title which is still used – 'The Ancient and Ornamental Woodlands'. Today, they are managed for conservation and amenity, not for timber production.

The Forest's 'important nature reserve status' was accepted by the Forestry Commission as early as 1949. In 1971 the entire New Forest was declared a Site of Special Scientific Interest. Natural England now takes a major role in many decisions concerning the management of the Forest.

The biological importance of the Forest has been recognised internationally by the provision of EU funds for the LIFE Project, which commenced in 1997. The purpose is to preserve and enhance biodiversity by removing scrub, repairing erosion, restoring damaged wetlands and the like.

Heritage Area & National Park

In the late 80s, a New Forest Heritage Area was defined, extending beyond the perambulation of the New Forest proper. This provided for closer consultation between the main bodies responsible for the management of the area. These include not only the Forestry Commission, the Verderers and Natural England, but also the County and District Councils, local landowners and other conservation agencies.

In 2005, the new Forest became Britain's smallest National Park, and the first one to be created in the South East. The objectives of the New Forest National Park Authority are to '*conserve*

Deer

The commonest species is the fallow deer, with up to 1,000 in the Forest. Their coat is dark in the winter, but chestnut with white spots in the summer. About a hundred of the much larger red deer frequent the woods and heathlands, with a small semi-domesticated herd at Burley. Around sixty sika deer, a Japanese species, live mainly in woods to the

east of Brockenhurst. The small roe deer are sometimes seen by those who make a point of walking quietly in the woods; there are about 300 of them. The muntjac, another 'foreign invader', is tiny and very rarely seen.

Riding stables cater for visitors wishing to see the Forest from horseback

Gorse in bloom on Furzley Common, Bramshaw

Foraging pigs disturb the ground in their search for tasty roots

and enhance the natural beauty, wildlife and cultural heritage' of the area, at the same time promoting the 'understanding and enjoyment of the Park's special qualities by the public'. The Authority has a significant new budget to achieve these objectives, which should be to the considerable benefit of the Forest.

However, the Authority will need to avoid the potential conflict between its two aims – pressure from increased visitor numbers could detract from, rather than enhance, the natural beauty. It is perhaps inevitable that some of the Authority's early proposals have caused controversy when so many different interests have a stake in the future of the Forest.

Habitats & landscapes

Almost any walk in the Forest will take the visitor through several different habitats, with the chance of seeing a variety of wildlife. This section can be no more than a brief summary of the various habitats.

The Ancient & Ornamental Woodlands

As early as 1877, Parliament recognised the need to preserve the 'picturesque character' of these unfenced woodlands, where domestic stock can wander at will. 'Pasture woodland' is a very unusual habitat, even on a European scale.

Deep in an area of A&O Woodland, the visitor is transported back to a landscape from medieval England. One would hardly be surprised to see a Norman king and his retinue pursuing their quarry through one of the open glades! The deer themselves are most likely to be seen early or late in the day.

Oak and beech dominate in the A&O Woods, often with a shrub layer of holly and sometimes hawthorn. While the woods are attractive at any time of year, the beeches in particular become a riot of brown, yellow, gold and russet in the late autumn. A vast range of fungus species appears at this time of year; ferns, mosses and lichens are also common.

As trees are allowed to live out their natural life-span and fallen trees are cleared only if they obstruct paths and

tracks, there is plenty of old, dead and decaying timber. This provides homes for beetles and other insects, which in turn become food for a variety of birds. Woodpeckers, treecreepers and nuthatches are common, along with many other species of woodland birds and predators like owls and hawks. Badgers are also common but rarely seen by the casual visitor.

Hardwood inclosures

Inclosures are planted woodlands, fenced to keep out domestic livestock. In the days before fencing, they were enclosed by earth banks, topped with dense plantings of thorny shrubs. Traces of these banks remain in many places in the Forest. Before 1851, species planted were mainly oak with some beech and sweet chestnut.

Grassy tracks through the woodland,

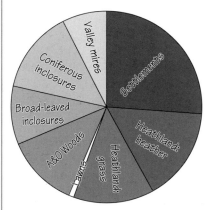

This diagram shows the approximate proportion of the different habitats within the Forest perambulation. This covers an area of 145 square miles (375 sq km). The New Forest National Park covers 220 square miles (571 sq km)

known as rides, are the best areas for wild flowers, especially in the spring. Dog violets and the yellowish-green heads of wood spurge are particularly common. Oak, bramble, honeysuckle, ivy and even some grasses are the food plants of numerous butterflies – meadow browns, various skippers and fritillaries, commas and so on.

Coniferous inclosures

Conifers became the norm for forestry plantation after the 1851 Act, but few have been planted since 1977. Most are not native British species, Norway spruce, Corsican pine and Douglas fir having been chosen by the Forestry Commission for their speed of growth, becoming mature in as little as fifty years.

Wildlife is generally less numerous in coniferous woodland than in hardwood areas. However, some birds such as siskins, crossbills and red-polls, and some fungi, prefer this habitat. Tall heaps of pine needles under the trees are the nests of wood ants.

In any of the woodlands, the most frequently seen mammal is the grey squirrel. This introduced North American species is not generally welcomed by foresters, as it strips the bark from young trees.

The Forestry Commission has a 100-year plan to replace gradually nearly all of the conifer plantations by deciduous woodland or even heathland.

Open heathland

Some areas of heathland are dominated by one or more of the three species of heather found in the Forest. Others are mainly composed of rough grasses. The dominant vegetation is often broken up by stands of bracken and clumps of gorse bushes (see pp.15 & 23).

Gorse, known locally as 'furze', produces masses of brilliant yellow pea-flowers mainly in the spring and early summer. But there are some flowers on the gorse, whatever the time of year. As the local saying goes:

'When furze is not in bloom
Kissing is out of season !'

Many people are surprised to see ponies and donkeys nibbling happily on the prickly gorse. Both gorse and heather are deliberately burnt in patches on a regular cycle, ensuring that there is always a supply of fresh young shoots which are more palatable than old ones.

Trees growing on the heathland include Scots pine, which was first planted in the Forest in 1776 and now seeds itself; rowan or mountain ash; crab apple, and silver birch.

Flowers include the tiny yellow tormentil, purple lousewort and a variety of orchids. Some are found only in limited areas, but the small heath spotted orchid is commonly seen. The greatest floral treasure of the New Forest is the carefully protected wild gladiolus, which grows nowhere else in Britain. It is rarely seen by the casual visitor, flowering in early summer under fronds of bracken.

The most distinctive bird of the heathland is the Dartford warbler, which is uncommon in other parts of the country. Stonechats are common, while linnets and a number of woodland species nest in gorse thickets.

Ponies cooling off in the Latchmore Brook, Ogdens, near Fordingbridge

The Forest is home to all six British species of reptile – adder, grass snake, slow-worm, common lizard, as well as the rare smooth snake and sand lizard. The presence of the adder, Britain's only poisonous snake, alarms some visitors. But an adder is very sensitive to vibration and will normally move away long before footfalls reach the spot where it is sunning itself. However, in

Eyeworth Pond near Fritham is a popular spot with walkers and cyclists

Riding through the stunning
New Forest

spring, when they have just emerged from hibernation, they may be too sluggish to move out of the way. This is another good reason to stay on paths and not to tramp through vegetation.

Forest lawns

A 'lawn' in the New Forest is not a patch carefully tended with a lawn-mower! – but an area of grass kept short by the numbers of ponies and cattle which regularly graze on it. Most lawns are quite natural, but a number result from deliberate re-seeding in the 1940s and 1950s, in some cases on former World War II airfields.

Though the lawns form only a small proportion of the overall area of open land, they are extremely important, especially those alongside streams, as they provide the best grazing in the Forest. Plants other than grasses are limited to those resistant to grazing pressure, including daisies, plantains and clover.

Valley mires

The valley mires of the New Forest, 'bogs' to most people, may be unattractive to walkers and sometimes dangerous for livestock, but in terms of biological diversity they are of incalculable value. There are around ninety separate mires, un-spoilt by drainage or any form of 'land reclamation', within the Forest. They probably represent well over half of all such habitats in the whole of Europe!

The plants of the mires are best observed where road bridges or foot-bridges cross the swampy land. The low bushy bog myrtle is common, as is the 'bog-moss', *Sphagnum*. Perhaps

the most fascinating of the bog plants are the different species of the insectivorous sundew. They compensate for the lack of nutrients in the damp peaty soil by using sticky hairs on their leaves to catch insects, which they digest. Nearby, the yellow bog asphodel often grows. The boggy land alongside some streams supports a dense growth of alder trees.

Siskins and redpolls feed on the seeds of the alder, while the insect life of the mires includes several species of dragonflies and their more slender relatives, the damselflies.

Streams and ponds

The largest of the streams which flow through the Forest are the Lymington River and the Beaulieu River. Other smaller watercourses go by such delightful names as Dockens Water and King's Garn Gutter.

In a few places, the water flow is slow and muddy stream beds have developed, allowing water plants to grow. But in most places the beds are gravelly and the flow quite strong, especially after rain, so few plants can live in the streams. Fishes such as minnows, sticklebacks and even trout thrive; they attract kingfishers, which nest in holes in the stream banks, and herons, which have a heronry at Sowley Pond.

This pond is the largest in the Forest but is on private land. Other relatively large ponds include Hatchet Pond and Eyeworth. There are many smaller ponds, some created especially to provide water for commoners' stock.

Mallards, teal and other water-birds, damselflies and dragonflies, frogs, toads and newts all frequent the ponds in varying numbers.

The coastal fringe

The Forest perambulation meets the waters of the Solent between the mouths of the Lymington and Beaulieu Rivers. Much of the coastline, however, is occupied by private land-holdings. The mud-flats and salt-marshes, with their distinctive saline-tolerant flora and numerous sea-birds and waders, are better appreciated on the nature reserves and public paths to the west of Lymington.

Farms, estates & villages

About a quarter of the area of the Forest is occupied by villages, farms, small-holdings and private estates, of which the largest is the Beaulieu Estate. Many of the land-holdings, of course, are occupied by the commoners who own the depastured* stock – which continues to graze on roadside verges and other open spaces within the settlements. The commoners' holdings with their hedges, pastureland and cultivated fields add one more element to the complex and fascinating mosaic of habitats which make up the New Forest.

* *See* 'Glossary - New Forest Words', p.106.

Ponies, Commoners & Agisters

For many visitors, the most characteristic feature of the New Forest is the presence of free-ranging ponies. They are encountered on open heathland and lawns, in the depths of the ancient woodlands – and on the roadsides, where they are at risk from careless drivers who ignore the necessary 40mph (64kph) speed limit.

Not everyone realises at first that the ponies are not 'wild'. Their owners, known as commoners, are all occupiers of holdings to which the Common Right of Pasture is attached. There are about 350 active commoners today with an average of around ten ponies each (see box on p. 25).

Commoning as a way of life is essential to the survival of the Forest; without the grazing animals the unenclosed habitats would change drastically. Unfortunately, there are many factors acting against commoning,

New Forest Ponies

The New Forest pony is a hardy breed and most of them remain on the open forest all winter, using gorse and woodland for shelter in the worst weather. Each group of ponies tends to have its own distinct area, and rarely wanders outside it. In the heat of summer, mixed herds of ponies, cattle and sometimes donkeys gather together in particular spots, known as 'shades'. Ironically, these often have no shade from the sun. It is believed that the stock are less troubled by biting insects in these areas. The position of a shade remains established over many generations – and some overlap modern motor-roads.

© Marion O'Neill

© Paul Close

Above: Heath spotted orchid, Beaulieu Heath

Above Right: The leaves of sundew have sticky hairs to trap insects

Right: New Forest Tour Bus

View of the heathland

including the general downturn in agricultural income. Few have ever expected to make a complete living from commoning and many commoners have other jobs.

Because of the desire of 'outsiders' to live in the Forest, properties (which incidentally have common rights attached) often command a market price well above that which intending commoners can afford. However, those brought up in the Forest generally feel a very strong incentive to continue in the traditional way of life, while the New Forest Council has policies to encourage the continuation of commoning.

The health of the ponies and other stock – and dealing with those injured or killed on the roads – is the responsibility of the six Agisters, paid officials employed by the Verderers. The Forest

The heathland is at its most colourful in August when heather is in bloom

Relaxing by the water

is divided into five areas, with an Agister responsible for each, while the Head Agister covers the whole Forest. Each pony has its tail clipped into a pattern which indicates to which area it belongs.

From August to November, the Agisters organise around forty-five 'drifts'. Local commoners, on horseback, round up the ponies in a limited section of the Forest and collect them in a temporary paddock or pound. Each pony is checked and dosed against worms. Some, at their owners' request, are fitted with reflective collars to reduce the risk of night-time road accidents.

Young foals are branded with their owner's mark, and each animal is tail-marked. The fee, which each commoner pays to the Verderers to depasture the pony, is known as the 'marking fee'. Once all of this has been done, many of the ponies are released. The rest are taken away by their owners in horse-boxes, perhaps destined for the next Pony Sale on the heathland near Beaulieu Road Station. All young colts are removed from the open Forest, as, in order to maintain the quality of the New Forest breed, only registered stallions are allowed to breed with the mares.

Keepers, Foresters & Rangers

The post of Keeper goes back to the time of the Norman kings. The Forest was then divided into 'walks', with one keeper responsible for the royal deer in each walk. Today, there are twelve sections, called beats, and the keepers are employed by the Forestry Commission. Each keeper lives in a cottage within his beat, often deep in the woods – and he is still responsible for the deer in his area.

With no natural predators in the Forest today, deer numbers have to be controlled or they would soon outstrip the food supply. Each spring's cull is carefully planned to maintain a balance of ages and sexes within the population. Thus the keepers, who carry out the cull, have to be expert shots. A keeper is knowledgeable, not just about the deer, but about all the wildlife in his beat. Keepers work with the foresters to ensure that forestry operations do not interfere with the interests of wildlife.

Over one hundred people are employed in commercial forestry. Conifers are the most important crop, with only about ten per cent of the timber being hardwood from broad-leaved trees. It takes fifty to sixty years before young conifers are ready for felling, although some wood is produced when twenty-year-old plantations are thinned. On each working day through the year, the foresters produce the equivalent of eight lorry-loads of wood. Timber from the Forest is used mainly in building and fencing, while twenty-five per cent becomes paper pulp or chipboard.

The ranger service was introduced in the early 1990s as the 'public face' of the Forestry Commission. The six rangers run a programme of walks and other events for the public (see 'Guided Walks' in the FactFile p. 107). They are also responsible for recreational activities, introducing school groups to the Forest and other educational ventures.

Common Rights in the New Forest

Common rights have existed as long as the Forest and are linked, not to individuals, but to land holdings.

The Right of Common Pasture

This is the most important of the common rights, both for the commoners and for the maintenance of the Forest environment. Without the cattle and ponies which graze in the New Forest, heathland would turn to scrub and scrub to woodland. Animal numbers fluctuate over the years, but in 1999 there were around 2,300 cattle, 3,400 ponies and 70 donkeys depastured in the Forest.

The Common Pasture of Sheep

Sheep are sometimes seen in the Forest, as a few holdings have the right to graze them, mainly around Bramshaw and Godshill.

The Right of Common Mast

Mast refers not just to beech-nuts, but also to unripe acorns which fall in great numbers in the autumn. If cattle or ponies eat too many, it can make them ill. But pigs love them and thrive on them. So, for sixty or more days each year, the pannage season, around a hundred pigs roam the Forest. They are most frequently seen on the Bramshaw Commons, where the right exists throughout the year.

The Right to Fuelwood or Estovers

At one time, the collection of wood for fuel was essential for most Forest dwellers. Only around 70 holdings still retain the ancient right of Estovers, and their firewood is now cut for them by the Forestry Commission, the commoners having to arrange collection.

The Right to Common Marl

This right, which is no longer used, was to extract limy clay from pits in the Forest. Before the use of fertilisers, clay was used to improve sandy soils in cultivated areas. It was also an ingredient of cob, once an important building material.

The Right of Turbary

The right to cut 'turf' (or peat) for use as fuel is no longer practised.

Bracken and Heather

Though not formal rights, many commoners once cut bracken and heather, practices which have almost died out. The heather was used for thatching outbuildings and even under the main thatch of cottages. The bracken, locally known as 'fern', made excellent animal bedding. Today the Forestry Commission keeps this invasive plant under control by cutting for compost; it makes an excellent peat substitute for gardeners.

Left: The New Forest Centre
Below: Horses on the road
Opposite Page: A much-photographed cottage at
Swan Green, Lyndhurst

Lyndhurst

All visitors to the Forest should spend some time in Lyndhurst, if only to visit the New Forest Museum. The village also caters for many other needs, with shops supplying books, maps, provisions, camping equipment, and many types of gifts and souvenirs. There is also a wide range of tea-rooms, pubs and restaurants.

Although a village, Lyndhurst has always been considered the 'capital of the New Forest'. At the time of the Domesday Book (1086), when the name was spelt 'Linhest', it was in the hands of the king. It is here that the Verderers' Court meets, and where the New Forest District Council, the Forestry Commission and the National Park Authority all have their offices.

The museum in the **New Forest Centre** tells the story of the Forest through a series of well-arranged displays and dioramas. As well as local history and traditions, it also deals with local characters, habitats and wildlife, the commoning way of life and forestry management, all in a manner which attracts children as well as informing adults.

A special feature is the New Forest Embroidery, created in 1979 to commemorate the nine hundredth anniversary of the New Forest. The concept was inspired by the Bayeux Tapestry and covers all the main historical events over nine hundred years, also illustrating the Forest's flora and fauna.

Victorian church

The **Parish Church of St Michael and All Angels** is an imposing Victorian brick structure dating from the 1860s. The fine east window contains stained glass considered *'infinitely superior to anything done by anyone else at that time'* (Pevsner, '*The Buildings of England – Hampshire*'). It was the work

New Forest Centre

The New Forest Centre, Lyndhurst, is packed full of displays and activities. There is something for all ages to enjoy

The centre includes:

The **New Forest Museum**, displays and activities about the New Forest National Park, it's history and traditions.

The **New Forest Gallery**, with a changing programme of exhibitions and displays.

The centre also houses a Visitor Information Centre, Reference Library and Gift Shop with local crafts.

It is the ideal place to start any visit to the New Forest National Park.

of Edward Burne-Jones and William Morris; the church has several other links with the pre-Raphaelite school of artists.

Behind the altar is a fresco of the 'Wise and Foolish Virgins' by Lord Leighton. When he painted this in 1862, he charged only for the cost of his materials, as he was trying out a new method of wall-painting intended to survive English weather conditions. It is said that local 'ladies' were the models for the wise virgins, while poorer women posed as the foolish virgins!

Queen's House

Not far from the parish church is **Queen's House**, always known as King's House when a king is on the throne. This was formerly the residence of the Lord Warden of the Forest, but now houses the offices of the Forestry Commission, with the ancient Verderers' Hall at one end. Part of the building dates from as early as the fourteenth century, but much of what we see today was added at the time of the Stuart monarchs.

The arched doorway, facing the road at the eastern end of Queen's House, is the entrance to the court-room used ten times a year for open sessions of the Verderers' Court, which is not otherwise open to the public. (See p. 38.)

Bolton's Bench & Swan Green

One of Lyndhurst's two cricket pitches, near the Beaulieu road, has a thatched pavilion. It is overlooked by **Bolton's Bench**, a hillock crowned with a distinctive growth of yew, with seats beneath. It was named after Lord Bolton, Lord Warden of the Forest in 1688.

Alice in Wonderland

On the south side of the churchyard is the simple tomb of the local Hargreaves family, much visited as the **'tomb of Alice in Wonderland'**. Alice Liddell of Oxford, the inspiration for Lewis Carroll's Alice, married Reginald Hargreaves and lived much of her life at Cuffnells House, Lyndhurst. A memorial inside the church commemorates two of her sons killed in the First World War.

At the other end of the village, by the Christchurch road, the second cricket pitch is on **Swan Green**. Named from the Swan Inn which it overlooks, this is one of the most picturesque village scenes in Hampshire. Photographs of the immaculate thatched cottages adjacent to the green must have featured on many postcards and biscuit tins!

With five traffic routes meeting at Lyndhurst, the approaches to the village often have long traffic queues at peak times, despite a one-way circulation. (As any route for a by-pass would involve damage to New Forest habitats, all proposals have been rejected.) The next section considers a number of short excursions, radiating out from Lyndhurst. They could be undertaken on bicycles, perhaps hired from **AA Bike Hire** in Gosport Lane, though fast motor roads are included in some routes.

Around Lyndhurst

There are extensive areas of woodland to the south of Lyndhurst, which are easily reached from Clayhill car park on the east of the A337 Brockenhurst road, and Whitley Wood car park (no dogs) on the west. On the same road, almost 3 miles (2km) from the village, is the entrance to New Park. This is home to the largest annual event in the area, the New Forest Show (See p.31).

A short distance from Swan Green is the hamlet of **Emery Down** and the New Forest Inn, a popular pub with an interesting history. Ale was originally sold here, around 200 years ago, from a caravan. Extensions were added till it became a permanent building, with part of the original caravan structure still at the heart of it today!

Taking the left turn by the pub, a minor road leads through woodland and after 3 miles (5km), reaches Bolderwood car park (see Ringwood chapter). On the way, shortly after **Millyford Bridge car park**, there is a strange structure, set a little way back on the left of the road. This is the '**Portuguese Fireplace**'.

During World War I a detachment of the Portuguese Army worked as lumberjacks in this area, cutting timber which was transported across the channel for building trenches, huts and walkways. The fireplace was the only stone structure in their hutted camp and remained as a memorial after the rest was demolished.

Minstead

Taking the A337 road north out of Lyndhurst, a left turning after 1¼ miles (2km) leads to the scattered village of **Minstead**. The pub and the church are both near the small central green, and both are of interest.

The pub is **The Trusty Servant**; its sign is a copy of an original painting in Winchester College dating from around 1600. According to the artist, the qualities of an ideal servant would be: the body of a pig (which will eat anything), the feet of a stag (for swiftness) and the ears of a donkey (for patience). The pig's snout is locked for secrecy and the creature holds the tools of his trade, a shovel, a brush and a pitch-fork.

All Saints' Church has a rather strange shape, the south transept being longer than the nave! The Georgian-style interior furnishings are unusual, with box pews and galleries, the highest of which, reserved for the poor, was

Lyndhurst, Brockenhurst & Around

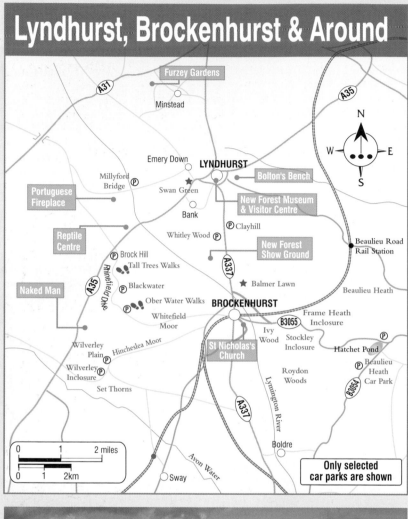

Furzey Gardens

Minstead

A31

A35

N
W E
S

Emery Down

LYNDHURST

Millyford Bridge Ⓟ

Bolton's Bench

Swan Green

Portuguese Fireplace

New Forest Museum & Visitor Centre

Bank

Ⓟ Clayhill

Reptile Centre

Whitley Wood Ⓟ

New Forest Show Ground

Beaulieu Road Rail Station

Ⓟ Brock Hill

Tall Trees Walks

A337

Naked Man

A35

Rhinefield Drive

Ⓟ Blackwater

★ Balmer Lawn

Beaulieu Heath

Ober Water Walks

BROCKENHURST

Whitefield Moor

B3055

Frame Heath Inclosure

Wilverley Plain

Hincheslea Moor

St Nicholas's Church

Ivy Wood

Stockley Inclosure

Hatchet Pond

Ⓟ

Ⓟ Beaulieu Heath Car Park

Wilverley Inclosure Ⓟ

Roydon Woods

B3054

Set Thorns

Lymington River

A337

Boldre

0 1 2 miles

0 1 2km

Avon Water

Sway

Only selected car parks are shown

Cricket on Swan Green, Lyndhurst

New Forest and Hampshire County Show

Follow special traffic signs from Lyndhurst or Brockenhurst

Many horse events, rings for cattle and sheep, flower show, dog show, hundreds of trade stands, craft show, exhibits by Forestry Commission and other organisations, etc. Generally held every year on the last Tuesday, Wednesday and Thursday of July. Ring events from 8am each day.

For more information ☎ 01590 622409 or visit the website: www.newforestshow.co.uk

Jamie Squibb's bike stunt

Above & Left: There are lots of activities for children

Below: Pig Racing

Conan Doyle

Sherlock Holmes aficionados will be interested in a tombstone under an oak tree at the southern end of the churchyard. Sir Arthur Conan Doyle died in Sussex in 1930 and was later re-buried here, near his former home at Bignell House, Minstead. His book '*The White Company*' (1891) is largely set in and around the Forest.

known as the 'gypsies' gallery'. The pew once reserved for the owners of Castle Malwood house has its own fireplace! There is also a three-tier pulpit; box pews meant that the preacher had to be high up in order to be seen. The second tier was used by lay-readers and the lowest tier by the clerk.

Near the south-west end of the church is the intriguing tomb of Thomas Maynard, who died in 1807. It bears a carving of the old wind instrument known as a serpent; Thomas had probably played in one of the church bands, which were common before the introduction of organs.

Just to the east of the main path is the memorial stone for Thomas White, initially described as a 'faithful husband'.

But his widow began to hear stories and had the word 'faithful' removed – leaving a very obvious rectangular space on the stone!

Furzey Gardens

A short distance away, around Minstead's network of lanes, is **Furzey Gardens**. It is connected with a charity that provides horticultural training for young people with learning disabilities, and plants grown by the students are on sale in the nursery shop.

There is botanical interest here all the year round, with a lake, a fernery, a heather garden, rhododendrons and azaleas, as well as Chilean fire trees and a 'bottle-brush tree'.

There are two thatched buildings

within the cottage-style gardens. **Forest Cottage** is believed to be well over 400 years old. Visitors can wander in and admire the open hearth, the bread-oven and other features – an opportunity to obtain a real feel of how life was once lived in the Forest. Nearby is the **Will Selwood Art and Craft Gallery**.

New Forest Reptile Centre

Three miles (2km) from Lyndhurst on the A35 Christchurch road, a gravel track leads off to the right. The **Reptile Centre** at Holidays Hill is a free facility provided by the Forestry Commission to give visitors a chance to see some of the more elusive wildlife of the Forest. All the species of reptile and amphibian which live in the wild in Britain – snakes, lizards, frogs, toads and newts – are housed here in eight open-air pens.

To the south-west of Lyndhurst, accessible either by Pinkney Lane or from a turning off the Christchurch road about half-way to the Reptile Centre, is the little village of **Bank**,

The New Forest Reptile Centre

with its popular traditional pub, The Oak. A short walk into the woodlands from here is the very unusual settlement of **Gritnam**. In this hamlet, each cottage has its garden, but there are no fields or paddocks – the whole place is incredibly compact for an ancient settlement.

A story passed down in a local family tells of how a Queen (which Queen was not specified), riding through the Forest, tore her clothing. A Gritnam villager mended it for her and as a reward the Queen gave permission to enclose from the Forest as much land as the family could dig in a specified time. No-one bothered to dig, the permission lapsed and so Gritnam remained the same size!

Brockenhurst & Around

Brockenhurst, 4 miles (6.5km) south of Lyndhurst on the A337, is the largest of the New Forest villages. Within a short distance, there are several Forestry Commission waymarked walks. For visitors not inclined to map-read their way into the depths of the Forest, these walks provide an excellent means of seeing some of the natural habitats.

Brockenhurst

The name 'Brockenhurst' is traditionally said to mean 'badger's wood'. However, 'broken wooded hill' may be a more likely interpretation – broken in the sense of divided by the valleys of streams. Records say that, in the twelfth century, the Manor was held by Peter Spilman. In return, he had to provide litter for the King's bed and hay for

Roe deer leaping at Blackwater. If you keep your eyes open you can often be rewarded by the unexpected

Left: Cow crossing the road. The speed restrictions help to prevent potential incidents

Below: Sows and piglets are often seen in the Bramshaw area

Autumn tints are often rewarding, so ensure you have your camera!

'Brusher' Mills

The tomb of Harry Mills, better known as **'Brusher' Mills**, is in the graveyard of the parish church, St Nicholas. His nickname came from his practice of brushing Brockenhurst cricket pitch before a match to remove twigs and leaves – and, no doubt, animal droppings. But his main claim to fame was that he made his living by catching snakes in the Forest, apparently immune to the bite of an adder.

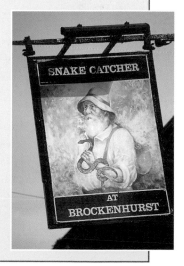

He prepared a primitive anti-snakebite serum from the snakes themselves, despatching any spare specimens to London Zoo as food for secretary birds and the like. He was not averse to earning gratuities from visitors by capturing snakes which had suddenly appeared among them – snakes which he had surreptitiously released himself!

A carving on his tombstone shows the wattle and daub hut in which he lived in the depths of the Forest for the last twenty years of his life.

his horse, 'when the king should be at Brockenhurst'.

The main street, Brookley Road, has a reasonable number of specialist shops catering for locals and visitors alike. In spite of cattle grids, ponies sometimes wander through the shopping areas.

By the entrance to one of the two car parks stands a brick plinth. Attached to it is a 'wheel plate', a great disc of cast iron which was used until 1915 by the local forge when applying metal rims to wooden wagon wheels.

It is not unusual for minor roads in the Forest to pass through fords, though most are frequently dry. The most famous is the Brockenhurst 'waters-plash' at the western end of Brookley Road. Vehicles leaving the village for Rhinefield or Burley generally have to drive through a few inches of water here.

At the other end of Brookley Road, near the main-line rail station, are the **New Forest Cycle Experience** and three pubs, the Foresters Arms, the Morant Arms and the Snake-catcher. The latter name commemorates a famous local character who died in 1905, aged sixty-seven.

Heading south out of Brocken-hurst, there are sometimes traffic delays, due to level-crossing gates near the station. Shortly after, a lane to the left leads to **St Nicholas's Church**, (generally open for visitors between 2.30 and 5pm). The church is the oldest in the Forest and has a fine Norman doorway in the south porch. In the churchyard, near Brusher Mills' grave, there is, surprisingly, a New Zealand war cemetery. Neat rows of tombstones commemorate over one hundred soldiers who

Peterson's Tower

Sway's oddest claim to fame, and one which dominates the view from much of the open heathland nearby, is Sway Tower (situated on private land). Also known as **Peterson's Tower**, it was built in the 1880s by Andrew Peterson, a retired judge from British India. It is 218ft (66.5m) high and took five years to build, with the purpose of demonstrating the value of concrete as a building material. It is said that Peterson, a spiritualist, received architectural directions from none other than Sir Christopher Wren!

died in a nearby field hospital during World War I.

About half a mile (0.8km) southwards, on the Brockenhurst-Lyming-ton road (A337), is the Filly Inn. Just past the inn, down a short lane, a footpath leads to **Roydon Woods Nature Reserve**. While not within the perambulation of the New Forest, the landscape is similar – ancient woodland with some areas of meadow and heath. As grazing by domestic stock is carefully controlled, the reserve has a wider variety of plant life than many grazed areas in the Forest.

A short distance further along the A337, there is a right turning towards Sway. The first Forest car park on the left is by a pond reserved for the use of model yacht enthusiasts. The road continues across open heathland; a left turning leads to **Sway**.

Sway and Wilverley

The village of Sway is largely of post-railway age, but there are some

The 'Naked Man'

A feature known as the '**Naked Man**', marked on OS Maps, is situated near the northern edge of Wilverley Inclosure. It may be approached from Wilverley Plain car park or, as a shorter walk, from Wilverley Post on the A35. There is little to see today – the stump of a tree covered with ivy and protected by a fence. Not so long ago, it was a gaunt dead oak with two projecting branches like arms. Further back in history, when this track was part of the road to Burley, the tree had a sinister use. Smugglers and highwaymen were hanged here as a deterrent to others passing by.

Ober Water Walks

At the far end of the lawn is Whitefield Moor car park (toilets). This is the departure point for the **Ober Water Walks**, which give views of woodland, heathland, lawn and stream. There are two routes, one of 1 mile (1.5km) and one of 1½ miles (2.5km); they are way-marked in different colours and both are entirely on gravel paths.

older corners with thatched cottages. Captain Marryatt's Victorian novel, '*The Children of the New Forest*', was set in this area. Sway also boasts **Artsway**, an award-winning contemporary art gallery.

Leaving the village to the north, a minor road runs alongside Set Thorns Inclosure and across heath-land towards the level lawn of **Wilverley Plain**. Many animals gather here – the lawn provides much better grazing than heathland. During World War II, it was ploughed to supplement war-time food production. After the war, no longer needed to produce cereals and potatoes, it was re-seeded with grass and clover. Since then, the grassland has gradually reverted to a state similar to the completely natural lawns.

Wilverley Plain car park has public toilets while the nearby Wilverley Inclosure **car park** has a barbecue site (bookable). A 2½-mile (4.2km) waymarked walk through **Wilverley Inclosure**, suitable for accompanied wheelchairs and baby-buggies, may be started from either car park. This is a commercially managed woodland which produces around 1,000 tonnes of timber in a year. Nevertheless, the scene is quite varied, with young and mature conifers interspersed with sweet chestnut, oak and beech.

From Wilverley, a minor road leads directly back to Brockenhurst across

Seeing Stars

A piece of advice for city dwellers: make a point of visiting the open heathland, well away from towns and villages, on a clear night. Wait till your eyes have adjusted to real darkness, then look up at the stars. The New Forest is one of the few places in southern England where the full glory of the heavens is not hidden by street lamps.

The Verderers

Public sessions of the Verderers' Court take place ten times a year in the ancient Verderers' Hall at Lyndhurst

The Verderers' Court of Norman times had the function of protecting the 'vert' – the greenery of the Forest which provided food and cover for the king's deer. A commoner who shot a deer might be punished by the removal of a hand or even execution. Other offences included taking wood from the Forest and enclosing land without permission. Any dog which was too large to pass through the 'Crown Stirrup' had to be expeditated – partially lamed by the removal of toes, so that it was not fast enough to pursue deer.

The New Forest Act of 1877 re-constituted the Verderers' Court, which had largely lapsed by this time. Its new role was to protect the interests of the commoners. Today, the Verderers protect grazing rights and are concerned with the health of all the depastured stock. They employ the six Agisters and obtain income from marking fees paid by the commoners on their stock. The Official Verderer is appointed by the Crown; the Forestry Commission, DEFRA, the National Park Authority and Natural England each appoint one Verderer. The other five are elected by the registered commoners.

Importantly, development control comes within the Verderers' remit. Working in close co-operation with the Forestry Commission, they are involved in most of the management decisions affecting the open forest.

A meeting of the court, officially the 'Court of Swainmote and Attachment', is opened with a cry of 'Oyez, oyez, oyez!' from the Head Agister. Anyone with an interest in the Forest may make a presentment, perhaps something as simple as a request to enclose a small section of lawn to protect a village cricket pitch – or a far-reaching suggestion that more of the Forest roads should be fenced to reduce animal deaths. The Verderers generally give their decisions at the next open court.

Two ancient relics are preserved in the Hall. The 'Stirrup of Rufus' or 'Crown Stirrup' is of Tudor date; a replica may be seen in the New Forest Museum. An ancient oak structure which was formerly the prisoner's dock is used today as a podium for those making presentments.

Hincheslea Moor, where a network of footpaths may be used to explore the undulating heathland. This route returns to the village centre via the watersplash.

Ober Water & Rhinefield

The other road out of Brockenhurst, via the ford, crosses **Whitefield Moor**, which often attracts large numbers of ponies and cattle. Like Wilverley Plain, it was cultivated during World War II, then re-seeded.

Beyond Whitefield Moor, the road enters extensive woodlands. Drivers should take great care here, as there is often little room for two cars to pass. The nearby **Rhinefield House Hotel** was built as a private house in 1887, on the site of a much older Forest keeper's lodge. The gardens are restored to their 1890s design, while the interior features rooms based on Westminster Hall and the Alhambra Palace!

Rhinefield Drive was the private drive of the house until 1938 and had been planted with specimen trees in 1859 when it was fashionable for landowners to experiment with exotic tree species. They include Spanish fir, black spruce, red spruce, Lawson cypress, Weymouth pine, Wellingtonia and western red cedar. Several that have grown to maturity are thought to be the tallest of their kind in Britain.

Balmer Lawn & Hatchet Pond

On the northern outskirts of Brockenhurst, just off the A337 Lyndhurst road, stands the **Balmer Lawn** Hotel. The

Rhinefield Walks

The exotic tree species of Rhinefield Drive may be appreciated on the waymarked **Tall Trees Walk** (1½ miles (2.5km) which loops from Blackwater car park (toilets) to Brock Hill car park and back again.

A shorter alternative, the **Blackwater Arboretum Trail** (½ mile (0.75km) and suitable for wheelchairs) passes through an arboretum started in 1960, with specimens of many broad-leaved and coniferous trees. Interpretative panels suggest that visitors 'use their senses to discover the secrets that these trees hold'.

Sika deer

The Japanese sika deer which live in the Forest are mostly found in **Frame Heath Inclosure**. They are descended from a small group which escaped from Beaulieu Estate about a century ago, and at the 1999 'census' there were sixty-one individuals. They may frequently be seen from footpaths through the woods, especially early or late in the day.

'lawn' extends to about 200 acres (81 hectares) to the north and east of the hotel. At one time, New Forest ponies competed on a race-track here! Today, the visitor may explore the nearby inclosures on foot or on a bicycle from **Balmer Lawn Bike Hire**. The car park by the Lymington River is very popular in summer.

Just to the south of the hotel, the B3055 road leads towards Beaulieu. The first Forest car park, Ivy Wood, provides access to an area of oak woodland alongside the Lymington river. The road then passes between several inclosures.

The Brockenhurst-Beaulieu road comes out of the woods onto **Beaulieu Heath** by Stockley Inclosure car park, then runs more or less straight over the heathland to **Hatchet Pond**, the largest accessible body of water in the New Forest.

A short distance down the B3054 Lymington road from the pond is **Beaulieu Heath car park**. This level open heathland was commandeered for an airfield during World War II. Halifaxes and American Thunderbolts

Hatchet Pond

Hatchet Pond is a very popular spot, providing a scenic backdrop for picnics, plenty of ducks for children to feed and sometimes dramatic summer sunsets. The pond was created in the eighteenth century to provide water-power for an iron mill. 'Hatchet' is an old Forest term for a gateway through which ponies and cattle pass from private smallholdings into the Forest itself. The pond has a great deal of wildlife interest, of which the most spectacular are the white drifts of bog-bean flowers in late spring. Pike, perch, rudd, roach, bream, tench, carp and eels are all found here. (Car park; toilets; often an ice-cream van; fishing permits available.)

at times operated around the clock. Appropriately, a section of the old tarmac runway is set aside for enthusiasts to fly model aircraft.

Places to Visit

Artsway

Station Road, Sway near Forest Heath Hotel
☎ 01590 682260
Outdoor sculpture, temporary exhibitions, talks, events and workshops, working artists' studios; full disabled access. Open: 11am–5pm Tue to Sun.

Conan Doyle tombstone

Minstead, New Forest
The tombstone is under an oak tree at the southern end of the churchyard.

Furzey Gardens

School Lane, Minstead, Lyndhurst SO43 7GL
☎ 02380 812464
www.furzey-gardens.org
Informal gardens surrounding Forest Cottage; play cabins for children; art and craft gallery; refreshments; plant nursery; wheelchair access except cottage. Open: daily 10am–5pm Mar to Oct.

New Forest and Hampshire County Show

Follow special traffic signs from Lyndhurst or Brockenhurst
☎ 01590 622409
www.newforestshow.co.uk
Generally on the last Tue, Wed and Thur of July. Includes: horse events, rings for cattle and sheep, flower show, dog show, trade stands, craft show, exhibits by Forestry Commission and other organisations.

New Forest Centre

Central car park, Lyndhurst, SO43 7NY
☎ 023 8028 3444
www.newforestmuseum.org.uk
Museum of New Forest history and traditions; gallery with changing exhibitions, gift shop with local crafts; Resource Centre and Visitor Information Centre. Free entry for accompanied under 16s; full wheel-chair access. Open: daily from 10am–5pm.

New Forest Reptile Centre

Holidays Hill, Lyndhurst, off A35, 2 miles (3km) west of Lyndhurst
☎ 023 8028 3141
Eight open-air pens in a Forest clearing; display panels; rangers often on hand. Parking fee, no admission charge, Disabled access. Open: daily 10am–4.30pm Apr to Sept.

Roydon Woods Nature Reserve

Access from lane off the A337, just south of the Filly Inn
☎ 01489 774400
Ancient woodland rich in wild-life with some areas of both dry and wet heathland, keep to public footpaths. Information leaflet from Hampshire Wildlife Trust. Open at all times.

The Verderers of the New Forest

The Queen's House, Lyndhurst, SO43 7NH
www.verderers.org.uk
Public sessions of the Verderers' Court take place ten times a year in the ancient Verderers' Hall at Lyndhurst

This circular route from Fordingbridge takes in much of the north-western heathlands of the Forest and some areas of woodland. Beyond the perambulation, it also includes part of the Avon Valley and some villages of the 'Western Downland'.

Fordingbridge

Although **Fordingbridge** lost its market around 200 years ago, a triangular junction of three streets is still known as the Market Place. **St Mary's Church**, at the south end of Church Street, has a fine hammer–beam–style roof in its north chapel, dating from the fifteenth century.

At the north end of Salisbury Street stands the historic **Court House** dating from early in the eighteenth century. Manorial Courts of the Manor of Burgate were held here until at least 1886. Burgate Manor House itself stands on the other side of the town's by-pass and is occupied today by the Game Conservancy Trust, which advises landowners on pheasant-rearing

and the like.

The most photographed aspect of the town is the ancient seven-arch **Great Bridge**, best seen from the Recreation Ground. Standing beside the river on the north side of the bridge is a bronze statue by Sir Ivor Robert Jones. It represents the painter Augustus John, of bohemian reputation, who had his studio near Fordingbridge from 1928 till his death in 1961.

Fordingbridge has an excellent small **Museum**, off Salisbury Street, open in the summer months. At the other end of the town is **Branksome China**, offering interesting factory tours on weekends throughout the year.

As you leave Fordingbridge on the B3078, you pass the Augustus John pub – known as the Railway Hotel until the nearby line closed in 1963. One mile (1.5km) past the pub, take a road to the right, signposted Rockbourne.

Western Downland

Shortly before you reach the village, **Rockbourne Roman Villa** may be visited. It was excavated in the 1950s by a local enthusiast, A T Morley Hewitt; over fifty rooms were discovered. Today, low walls reveal the layout of the site and there are small mosaics and a hypocaust. The excellent museum displays some of the objects found in the excavation and shows many aspects of life in a Romano-British villa of the second to fourth centuries.

It is well worth continuing a short distance along the same road to visit the village of **Rockbourne**, which many consider one of Hampshire's prettiest. Thatched cottages line both sides of the village street, with a clear chalk stream running along one side.

A longer detour may be made, using

Rockbourne Roman Villa

Martin Down Nature Reserve

Adjacent to A354 Blandford road, 7 miles (11km) from Salisbury

Chalk grassland with a wide variety of wild flowers, butterflies, birds and other wildlife; network of footpaths. Information leaflet from Natural England.

minor roads via Damerham, to another interesting and once very remote village. **Martin**, then part of Wiltshire, featured in W H Hudson's *A Shepherd's Life*. The extensive open grasslands of the chalk downs, once grazed by vast numbers of sheep, are now mostly arable fields. An impression of the former appearance of this countryside may be gained by a visit to **Martin Down National Nature Reserve**. It is a habitat for a great variety of wild flowers and many different species of butterflies and birds.

Breamore & Woodgreen

Breamore may be reached from Rockbourne along narrow lanes, or by returning to Fordingbridge and taking the Salisbury road northwards. **Breamore House**, less than 1mile (1.5km) from the main road, is a fine Elizabethan manor house. Built in the 1580s, it passed into the hands of the Hulse family in 1748 and has been their family home ever since.

A guided tour through the main rooms of Breamore House reveals fine examples of period furniture, including a 400-year-old Jacobean bed. A collection of interesting works of art includes *The Boy with the Bat*, which may be the earliest representation of a crick-

eter. There is also, rather surprisingly, a gallery of Mexican ethnological paintings. A portrait of Christian Dodington, the wife of a former owner, is said to carry a curse – anyone who moves it out of its position in the Grand Hall will meet a sudden death soon afterwards!

The **Countryside Museum**, situated in the former walled garden of the house, has much to fascinate visitors of all ages – old farm tools and machinery, the reconstructed interior of a farmworker's cottage, a schoolroom, shops and various tradesmen's workshops. Nearby is Breamore's **Parish Church of St Mary**, considered a very fine example of Saxon architecture and believed to be at least 1,000 years old.

It is worthwhile spending some time in **Breamore** itself. (The author admits bias, having been brought up here!) The village has an extensive area of open grazing land, available to villagers, and many thatched cottages. Almost uniquely, there is no modern development, the village being designated a Conservation Area.

Just to the south of the Bat and Ball Hotel (with an inn sign inspired by *The Boy with the Bat*), a lane leads past Breamore Mill to the village of Woodgreen. **Woodgreen Common** is an attractive spot, with thatched cottages overlooking a Forest lawn with a cricket pitch.

However, the village's most interesting feature is **Woodgreen Village Hall**. Much of the interior surface of its walls is covered with murals painted in 1931 by two art students, both of whom became eminent men in later life. The scenes show aspects of village life and all of the people illustrated – Morris dancers, Sunday School pupils, apple-pickers, poachers, cricketers and so on – were local inhabitants at the time.

About 2½ miles (4km) north-east of Woodgreen (a possible detour around narrow twisting lanes) is the village of Hale, where picturesque thatched cottages adjoin **Hatchet Green**.

A minor road, starting just to the south of the Horse and Groom pub, leads out of Woodgreen towards Godshill. A short distance up the hill, an even more minor lane to the right leads to **Castle Hill**, which gains its name from a small Iron Age hill-fort at the far end of the ridge. The parking spaces here provide a superb view of the Avon valley.

The Woodgreen to Godshill lane passes between two inclosures, in either of which a pleasant woodland stroll may be enjoyed. Then the road descends into a valley and passes through a ford, generally dry but occasionally impassable after a downpour, before reaching the B3078 and the open Forest by the Fighting Cocks pub.

Godshill to Fritham

Soon after turning left towards Cadnam there is a car park by **Godshill cricket pitch**. This is a good spot to set out for a walk to Ditchend Bottom, Pitts Wood Inclosure and the woods and heathlands beyond. The gravel track starting from the next car park, Ashley Walk, leads onto a ridge where the dam-buster bombs were secretly tested in World War II.

The B3078 follows a heathland ridge to the road junction known as **Bramshaw Telegraph**. This is the second highest point in the Forest, 419ft (127m) above sea level. (Piper's Wait, less than a mile away, is 420ft (128m).) In the nineteenth century, signals were passed from the Admiralty to Plymouth by a chain of semaphore signalling stations. It was said that a time signal could reach Plymouth from London in forty-five seconds. No trace of the 'telegraph' remains, except in the name.

After 1½ miles (2.5km), there is a right turning to Fritham. On the nearby heathland is **Longcross Pond**, a favourite 'shading' spot for cattle and ponies. **Fritham** village has a patchwork of small fields, arranged in an almost radial pattern around the cottages, reminiscent of medieval village layout. Many of the inhabitants exercise their common rights.

Healing spring

A lane leads through the village, past the Royal Oak public house and down a hill to **Eyeworth Pond**. Near the point where a stream flows into the small lake, the ground is stained orange from the Chalybeate Spring. This is due to the iron contained in the water, which was considered to have healing properties. Eyeworth is an idyllically peaceful spot today, with ducks and water-lilies on the lake, but it was not always so (see picture p.18).

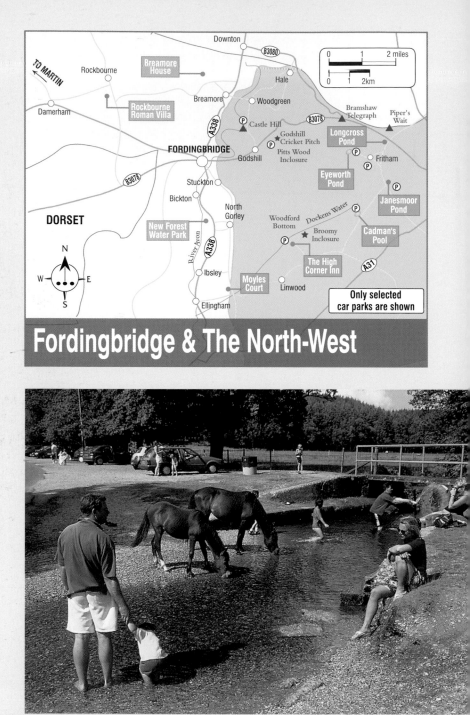

Fordingbridge & The North-West

Both children and ponies enjoy the ford and the stream near Moyles Court

Breamore House

The well-known view of the Avon Valley from Castle Hill, Woodgreen

Eyeworth Pond

Eyeworth Pond was created by damming a stream in 1871. Somewhat surprisingly, its purpose was to provide power for the Schultze gunpowder factory at nearby Eyeworth Lodge, which operated from 1865 till 1923.

The product was a 'smokeless sporting powder'. One of the ingredients was fine charcoal produced from the wood of local alder trees. (Alder charcoal was also made in the Forest in World War II and used in the filters of gas masks.) Over 100 local men were employed in the factory, at wages significantly above those paid to farm labourers at the time. They walked to work from many surrounding villages and were searched for matches at the gate. On at least one occasion, in August 1871, a worker died in an explosion, a sound like the firing of artillery being heard seven miles away in Fordingbridge.

Pools & streams

From Eyeworth, return through Fritham village and take the road south towards Stoney Cross. The first car park on the left is near **Janesmoor Pond**. Fishing here is limited to anglers under the age of fourteen; no permit is required. Continue along the road, once part of the runway of Stoney Cross airfield (World War II), then take a right turn, signposted Linwood.

About 1 mile (1.5km) beyond this turning, there is a car park by **Cadman's Pool**. Fishing is allowed here, with permit, though in the spring many visitors come to admire newly hatched ducklings and goslings. The name of the pond commemorates Arthur Cadman, who as Deputy Surveyor of the New Forest was responsible for the creation of this pond in the 1960s. (As the Queen holds the title Surveyor of the New Forest, the chief local official of the Forestry Commission is known as the Deputy Surveyor.)

The Linwood road continues across Ocknell Plain, turning right at a T-junction, and across Broomy Plain. About 2½ miles (4km) from Cadman's Pool, **High Corner Inn** is signposted down a gravel track to the right. The nearby High

Dame Alice Lisle

In 1685 Dame Alice Lisle, a 70-year-old widow, lived at Moyles Court. After the Battle of Sedgemoor, she innocently gave shelter to a fugitive from the Monmouth Rebellion. She was arrested for harbouring a traitor and was tried at the infamous 'Bloody Assize'. The notorious Judge Jefferies sentenced her to be burnt at the stake. Thanks to the intervention of the Bishop of Winchester, the sentence was 'commuted' to one of beheading, which was carried out on September 2nd in Winchester market-place. Alice Lisle's grave is in the parish churchyard at Ellingham; and a nearby public house now bears her name.

Corner car park is an excellent base for walkers to explore the valley of Docken's Water and Broomy Inclosure.

Moyles Court

The road then meanders through woods and heaths, through the small scattered settlement of Linwood, till it reaches a junction of minor roads near **Moyles Court**. On the lane leading north to Gorley, there is a well-known water-splash. Beside it stands an ancient tree called the 'Moyles Court Oak'. The spot is a popular family stopping place in summer, with children paddling in the stream. Moyles Court house, a fine mid-seventeenth century brick edifice, is now a private school and was the scene of an historic event (see box p.48).

Avon Valley

From Moyles Court, there are two routes north to return to Fording-bridge. The busy A338 runs near the River Avon, while the parallel minor road passes through the little Forest settlements of Ibsley, South Gorley, North Gorley and Stuckton. Each village has its common with grazing ponies; most were only brought within the Forest perambulation in 1964.

On the A338 at Blashford, about one mile north of Ringwood, former farm buildings have been converted into a fascinating museum called the **Town and Country Experience**. There are local finds of prehistoric, Roman and medieval artifacts and plenty of panels with old photographs concerning the history of the area. An upstairs room is devoted to links between the RAF and the various airfields which existed in the New Forest during World War

II. There is even, incredibly, an original 'Bouncing Bomb' like those tested on the heathlands not far away.

Several of Ringwood's shops of the early 20th century have been lovingly recreated, full of contemporary goods including toys, cameras and radios. Vintage cars include the actual 1941 Hillman Minx used in *Foyle's War* television series.

At **Ibsley**, the river runs adjacent to the major road. Among the thatched cottages nearby is the popular Old Beams Inn, with obvious cruck beams supporting its northern wall. A causeway leads across the flood plain of the Avon to the church at Harbridge. The meadows in the Avon valley have considerable wildlife interest and those adjacent to this causeway are the winter haunt of large numbers of Bewick's swans.

North of Ibsley, just off the A338, is the **New Forest Water Park**, where visitors have the opportunity to water-ski, jet-ski or aqua-ride on two lakes, formed when old gravel workings were returned to nature.

Hockeys Farm at North Gorley, on the minor road, is a conservation farm, with all the animals reared organically. A farm walk leads to a copse with a picnic area and bluebells and primroses in the spring; also to a deer park. Organic meat, including venison, and other produce are on sale in the farm shop – a must for anyone on a self-catering holiday!

Bickton Mill, on a loop road off the A338, just to the south of Fordingbridge, produced a widely acclaimed 'farinaceous baby food' during the nineteenth century. Most of the building is now converted to flats, but it also houses the shop of the adjacent trout farm.

Places to Visit

Rockbourne Roman Villa

Rockbourne, Fordingbridge, SP6 3PG
(off B3078)
☎ 0845 603 5635
Remains of large Villa; museum of
Roman life. Open; daily 10.30am–6pm,
Easter weekend to end-Sept.

Martin Down Nature Reserve

Adjacent to A354 Blandford road,
7 miles (11km) from Salisbury
☎ 01980 620485
Open at all times. Chalk grassland with
a wide variety of wild flowers, butterflies,
birds, other wildlife and a network of
footpaths.

Breamore House & Countryside Museum

Breamore, nr Fordingbridge, SP6 2DF
(signed off A338)
☎ 01725 512468
www.breamorehouse.com
Elizabethan Manor House and
Countryside Museum set in its own
beautiful parkland amid surrounding
farms and fields. The grandeur and
magnificence of the house has
changed little over the past 400 years.
Conducted tours of house; museum of
country life; tea-room and gift shop.
Open: April Tue, Sun, and Easter
Weekend; May to Sept Tue, Wed, Thur,
Sat, Sun.
House: 2.00pm–5.30pm
Countryside Museum: 1.00pm–5.30pm
Tea Barn: 12.00pm–5.30pm
Saxon parish church nearby (guide
book by the present author!)

Ringwood Town & Country Experience

Salisbury Rd, Blashford, Ringwood
Bh24 3PA
☎ 01425 472746
www.rtce.co.uk
Everything from prehistoric tools to
vintage cars; Victorian dairy, railway
station, period shops, wartime airfields
of the New Forest. All undercover,
disabled access on ground floor.
Gift shop. Café within museum and
adjoining bistro open to all. Combined
family tickets available with Liberty's.
Open: daily, Easter to end-Oct,
10am–4.30pm; Nov to Easter, Sun to Fri
10am–4.30pm

Woodgreen Village Hall

Woodgreen, near Fordingbridge
☎ 01725 512288
Murals of village life in the 1930s. Open
only by prior appointment.

Above Right: Traction engine at the Countryside Museum

Right: The parish church of St Mary's, Breamore

Loading the press to make New Forest Cider

Although Ringwood lies beyond the New Forest perambulation, it has always had close ties with the Forest. The tour described in this chapter also takes in the village of Burley, with its witchcraft and smuggling associations, and some of the most extensive and interesting woodlands in the Forest.

Ringwood

Ringwood's market charter was granted as long ago as 1226. Every Wednesday, the **Market Place** fills with tradesmen's stalls, selling ev-erything from fruit and vegetables, through meat and fish, to underclothes and hardware. Around the restored lamp standard which commemorates Queen Victoria's Golden Jubilee in 1887, an auctioneer sells a wide assortment of objects; bundles of vegetable plants, lawn-mowers, washing machines, typewriters and rabbit hutches are among the items that may be found here.

The site of the old cattle market is now the **Furlong Shopping Centre**, with the former seed merchant's premises, Frampton's Mill, housing a café and wine bar. In the middle of the precinct is a magnificent full-size bronze sculpture of a mare and foal.

The White Hart

Ringwood's Domesday name of 'Ringvede' probably signified a ford across a river – the Avon is a short distance to the west of the town centre. In the Market Place the **Original White Hart Inn** claims to be the first inn of that name, due to a supposed connection with King Henry VII.

A 'white hart' is a stag with an unusual creamy-white coat. The variation is rare, but such stags are sighted in the Forest from time to time – seen crossing the road at night, picked out in headlights, a white stag is very striking, almost ghostly.

After the Rebellion of 1685 and his defeat at the Battle of Sedgemoor, the Duke of Monmouth was captured near Ringwood. While imprisoned in a house in West Street, the Protestant Duke reputedly wrote to his Catholic uncle, King James II, asking for clemency, but he was later beheaded. The building which stands on the same spot today is known as **Monmouth House**.

The original White Hart

The tale tells that Henry VII was hunting in the New Forest with his courtiers and they picked on a white hart as their quarry. It was eventually cornered somewhere near Ringwood; but soft-hearted ladies in the party persuaded the king to spare the stag's life. It was released with a gold collar round its neck. The inn where the king dined that day was renamed the White Hart.

Unfortunately, the Ringwood inn's claim to be the 'Original' White Hart is questionable; an inn of that name in Southwark is mentioned in Shakespeare's 'Henry VI'. And the same story of the white hart and the gold collar was told by the Roman writer Pliny, concerning Alexander the Great!

Owls & Smugglers

The B3347 road leads south towards Christchurch. Less than one mile from the town centre, just past a filling station, turn left into Moortown Lane, then left again in to Crow Lane, where you will find **Liberty's Owl, Raptor and Reptile Centre**. The raptors – birds of prey including hawks, eagles and owls – are housed in a series of aviaries, while the reptiles are in large tanks inside a heated building.

The centre is run by a professional falconer, but it is named from its avian star, Liberty, a large Alaskan Bald Eagle. There are twice daily flying displays by the birds, and also an opportunity to handle some of the reptiles, for those who wish to do so.

Smuggling

Smuggling was a major occupation in the New Forest in the seventeenth and eighteenth centuries. Taxes, especially on goods like tobacco, tea and brandy, were so high that 'free trading' was practised by many otherwise respectable citizens, including even clergymen. Chewton Bunny, a narrow wooded valley running down to the sea between Highcliffe and Barton-on-Sea, was a very popular place for landing contraband. Burley was conveniently on the route inland from this spot. The Queen's Head at Burley was one of many places in and around the Forest used for temporary storage of the goods before they were taken on to Salisbury, Winchester or Southampton.

It is hardly surprising that farm labourers were prepared to risk capture by the excise men for transporting illicit goods by wagon or pack-horse – a labourer's wages were around eight shillings a week, whereas one night's smuggling could earn ten shillings.

Women also had a role to play. The story is told of 'Lovey' Warne who lived near Burley with her smuggler brothers. If the customs men were around, she would stand on a prominent hill wearing a bright red cape as a warning to the smugglers to lie low. But this was not enough excitement for her. At a time when ladies only ever rode side-saddle, she would tuck up her skirts and straddle her pony, with a keg of brandy on either side of the saddle.

Behind the scenes, Liberty's is also a rescue and rehabilitation centre for injured wild birds of prey. On leaving Liberty's, return to Moorland Lane and continue towards Burley – about 3½ miles (5.5km) distant. The lane crosses the Forest perambulation and heads across Vale Moor. The first of the Forest car parks on the left is **Smugglers' Road car park**. The old track known as the Smugglers' Road can be followed northwards towards Picket Post, along a ridge with views that include the hills of the Isle of Purbeck on a clear day. Unfortunately, beyond this point, much of the track parallels the A31 trunk road and the peace of the Forest is destroyed by traffic noise.

A little further on from Smugglers Road, there is an Iron Age hill-fort known as **Castle Hill,** just to the right of the road, with fine views from its ramparts. Continue through Burley Street to the main part of the village.

Burley, home of a white witch

Of all New Forest villages, **Burley** is the one that has most enthusiastically adapted itself to the needs of visitors. At peak times, when the coach park is full, the tiny village centre swarms with people. Ponies and donkeys wander the streets and car park. Donkeys have

(Continued on p.56)

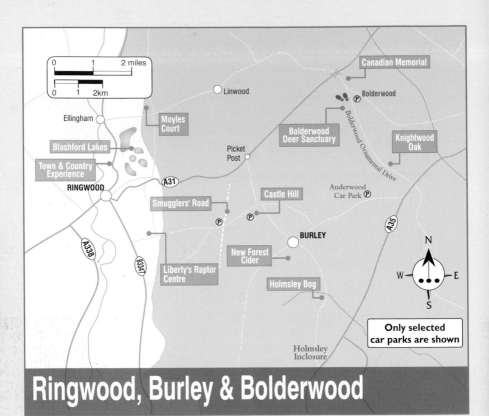

| 0 | 1 | 2 miles |
| 0 | 1 | 2km |

Linwood

Canadian Memorial

Bolderwood

Ellingham

Moyles Court

Bolderwood Deer Sanctuary

Bolderwood Ornamental Drive

Knightwood Oak

Blashford Lakes

Picket Post

Town & Country Experience

RINGWOOD

A31

Castle Hill

Anderwood Car Park

Smugglers' Road

A35

BURLEY

A338

B3347

New Forest Cider

Liberty's Raptor Centre

Holmsley Bog

Only selected car parks are shown

Holmsley Inclosure

N
W E
S

Ringwood, Burley & Bolderwood

A long-standing local tradition, the New Forest Foxhounds still meet regularly but have to obey current legislation about hunting with hounds (see box on p.56)

The Coven of Witches, Burley, former home of the white witch, Sybil Leek

One of the Forestry Commission's ten camp-sites

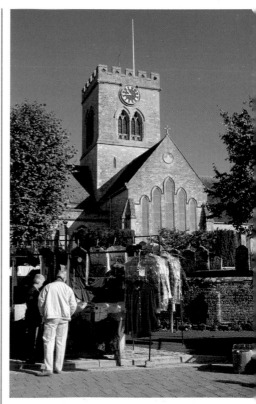

Ringwood Church and market

The hunt

The Queen's Head has had a long association with the hunt. Many 'sporting trophies' are displayed inside while hounds and huntsmen often meet outside.

After prolonged national controversy and debate, hunting with hounds was banned by Parliament in 2005. The New Forest Buckhounds had been voluntarily wound up in 1997.

Many Forest dwellers see the hunt as part of a centuries-old way of life, but the New Forest Foxhounds have had to modify the nature of their regular meets to abide by current legislation.

(See picture p.54).

been seen to block coach doorways in the hope that a passenger will pass out another mint-with-a-hole! – but visitors should never feed the Forest animals.

Tea-rooms and souvenir shops abound, several of the latter having a witchcraft theme. The explanation for this goes back only to the 1950s, when a well-known witch lived in Burley.

Sybil Leek was high priestess of a New Forest coven of 'white witches'. She was a familiar figure in the village, dressed in a long black coat with Mr Hotfoot Jackson, her pet jackdaw, perched on her shoulder.

She was famous for her healing herbal potions, and from her regular appearances on local television, reporting on the traditions of the New Forest.

So many visitors came to Burley to try to meet her that she emigrated to the USA. Her former home is now the shop known as 'Coven of Witches'.

Among the present-day attractions of Burley are the **Wagonette Rides**, which enable visitors to see something of the Forest at the pace of a good-tempered carthorse. Another way of exploring at a slower pace than the car is provided by **Burley Cycle Hire**. Fresh produce is always on sale at **Burley Fruit Farm**, adjacent to the main car park. Tractor-and-trailer rides are often run from the farm kiosk, with a guaranteed sighting of a small herd of red deer which live within a large fenced paddock.

Among the common rights attached to the premises of the **Queen's Head** pub is the Right of Turbary. Turf cut in the Forest was formerly burned in the open hearth of the pub, with bacon curing in the peaty smoke above.

Home-made cider

A little way from the village centre are the farm-yard premises of **New Forest Cider**. Cider-making was once a regular autumn occupation for many commoners, and the practice has been revived here. There is an ancient hand-operated ratchet press on display, but today's bulk production uses a modern hydraulic press.

Preparing the layers of apples, wrapped in cloths and sandwiched between slatted wooden trays, ready to transfer to the press, is still a labour intensive process. As the layers are compressed, the apple juice streams out. No water or other additives are used, just

Pollarded trees

In the past, many of the oak and beech trees in the Forest were pollarded. The word comes from the French 'poil' meaning to behead. A tree would be cut off at around 6-9ft (2-3m) from the ground and the leafy branches would be left for deer to browse. Later, the wood could be used as fuel. Over the years, the tree would grow again, but with a number of main branches where there was previously one trunk. The disadvantage was that it reduced the useful timber which was produced, especially for ship-building, so the practice was banned by parliament in 1698. Thus the many obviously pollarded trees in the Forest today are presumably all over 300 years old (see picture p.109).

yeast to start the fermentation.

To continue the circuit by the most direct route, leave Burley on the Lyndhurst road. About 3 miles (4.75km) from Burley, **Anderwood car park and picnic place** has toilets and a bookable barbecue area. The adjacent woodland includes many areas of young trees as, like several other parts of the Forest, this inclosure suffered considerable damage in the 'hurricane' of October 1987 and the almost equally devastating storm of January 1990. After another mile (1.5km), the A35 is reached; after less than half a mile (0.8km) on this road, turn left into Bolderwood Ornamental Drive.

As an alternative route to Bolderwood, take the Brockenhurst road out of the village, past the cricket pitch on the left. After a golf course on the right, take a minor road to the right and go a short distance downhill across Goatspen Plain. The OS Outdoor Leisure map gives one of the most intriguing of New Forest place-names here –'Anthony's Bee Bottom' – one whose origin is unfortunately lost in the mists of time.

Bogs & Inclosures

In the valley here, the road traverses Holmsley Passage, a causeway across **Holmsley Bog**. This is one of the largest and most biologically diverse of the New Forest mires, where over one hundred different species of plants are known to grow. Mires are treacherous places, for stock as well as for walkers, and are vulnerable to disturbance, so should be appreciated only from passages such as this.

Just beyond the passage there is an isolated building, which was a level-crossing keeper's dwelling on the former Southampton and Dorchester Railway – nicknamed 'Castleman's Corkscrew'. Castleman was the designer of the line which was one of the longest single-track lines in the country when opened in 1847. The epithet 'corkscrew' referred to the somewhat roundabout route which the track followed. (The former **Holmsley Station** is now a tea-room where the Burley-Brockenhurst road, part of which follows the old railway line, passes under the A35.)

(Continued on p.60)

New Forest Cider orchaid

Burley Wagon Rides

Fallow Deer

© CMJ Matthews

Forest trails

The **Deer Watch Trail** (½ mile/0.75km) takes in a viewing platform overlooking the **Bolderwood Deer Sanctuary** – take binoculars if you have them. The fallow deer which are often seen are just as wild as any of the other deer in the Forest. However, they tend to remain in these fields as the local keeper provides food for them daily, except in the autumn rutting season; so they are least likely to be seen here in October and November.

The **Jubilee Grove Trail** (1 mile/1.5km) passes the deer platforms and enters a grove planted in 1969 to commemorate the fiftieth anniversary of the founding of the Forestry Commission. Some fine trees remain from an ornamental arboretum planted around 1860.

The longest of the three routes, at 2 miles (3km), is the **Radnor Trail**, which goes deeper into the heart of the Forest and crosses the Bratley Water on two footbridges. Between a small swampy pond and the road is the **Radnor Stone**, a memorial to the seventh Earl of Radnor. For well over twenty years he was a very influential figure in the management of the Forest – a member of the Forestry Commission from 1942 till 1963, serving as Chairman for half that time, then the Official Verderer until 1966. Detailed carvings of New Forest wildlife ornament the sides of the stone.

The Radnor Stone

The road continues uphill beyond the former railway crossing and into **Holmsley Inclosure**. This is a pleasant place for a walk; there are both conifers and broad-leaved trees and consequently a variety of woodland birds. On leaving the inclosure, turn left onto the A35 Christchurch-Lyndhurst road; after 6 miles (10km), turn left into the **Bolderwood Ornamental Drive**.

Bolderwood

The Drive is a narrow unfenced road, a scenic route with ample opportunities to leave the car and to explore the magnificent adjacent woodlands on foot.

Only a short distance from the A35, the **Knightwood Oak** should be visited. This great pollarded oak is one of the oldest and largest trees in the Forest, believed to be around 500 years old. The picket fencing around it encloses the **Monarchs' Grove**. Eighteen oak trees were planted here in April 1979, one for each of the monarchs (listed on a plaque) known to have visited the New Forest since the time of William the Conqueror.

When the Queen and the Duke of Edinburgh came to the Forest for the Ninth Centenary celebrations in 1979, each planted a tree, not far from the Knightwood Oak. So far, the **Duke's Tree** is growing rather larger than the **Queen's Tree**.

Both **Barrow Moor** and **Mark Ash car parks** are excellent bases for exploring the ancient woodlands with numerous fine pollarded beeches. Barrow Moor can claim to be the centre of the Forest, being the furthest point from the perambulation in any direction.

Four miles (2.5km) from the A35 is **Bolderwood car park**, one of the most popular spots in the Forest. Toilets are provided, there are picnic tables in the adjacent wood and an ice-cream van is generally parked here. An area of lawn next to the car park is much used for family ball-games, even sunbathing when the weather is suitable. Thus many of those who park here never stray far from their cars. However, there are three way-marked forest walks starting from this car park, all on gravel paths and suitable for accompanied wheelchairs.

A short distance beyond Bolderwood car park is the **Canadian Memorial**. The Third Canadian Division was billeted in a tented camp here. For two months before the D-Day landings of 6th June 1944, open-air services for the troops were held in front of a wooden cross erected for the purpose. It remains as a memorial and wreaths are laid to commemorate those who died.

The road now traverses an area of heathland, then continues through an underpass. (It may not be clear on some maps that there is no access onto or from the A31 at this point.) Beyond Slufters Inclosure, the route joins that of the 'Fordingbridge and the Northwest' circuit, through Linwood to Moyles Court.

The 'Lake District'

Just to the south of Moyles Court, off the lane signposted Ringwood, is the Alice Lisle Inn. Nearby, part of the **Avon Valley Long Distance Path** gives access to the 'Ringwood lake

Places to Visit

Blashford Lakes Nature Reserve

Just off the A338, 1 mile (1.6km) north of Ringwood

A collection of lakes with large numbers of migratory wildfowl in the winter months. Occasional guided walks led by warden of Study Centre. Information leaflet available from Hampshire Wildlife Trust ℅ 023 8061 3636. Footpaths are open at all times; to book hide over-looking Ivy Lake ☎ 01425 472760

Burley Wagon Rides

From Queen's Head car park, Burley
☎ 0771 2074486
www.burleywagonrides.co.uk
Horse-drawn wagon rides lasting from 20 minutes upwards, booking advisable at busy times. Open: from 11am, Easter to Oct; not in wet weather. Dogs welcome.

Liberty's Owl, Raptor and Reptile Centre

Crow Lane, Ringwood, BH24 3EA
☎ 01425 476487
www.libertyscentre.co.uk
Many birds of prey to be seen in aviaries and during falconry displays; heated reptile house. Falconry Experience Days bookable in advance. Gift shop and small café, picnic area, full disabled access, Parking. Open: daily, Mar to Oct 10am–5pm; weekends only from Nov to Feb 10am–4pm.

New Forest Cider

Pound Lane, Burley, BH24 4ED
☎ 01425 403589
www.newforestcider.co.uk
Forest holding with Commoners' Rights, practising traditional cider-making; farm animals for children to see; local preserves and crafts in shop. Open for sale of cider at most times, including evenings and weekends; Cider pressing weekends available, call or visit the website for details.

district', an area of former gravel pits, flooded and returned to nature. (The path as a whole runs 26 miles (42km) from Salisbury to Christ-church.)

Several of the lakes constitute **Blashford Lakes Nature Reserve** which has a study centre used by schools and a hide for the use of keen bird-watchers. In winter, gadwall, goldeneye, shoveler, pochard, wigeon and other ducks gather here in large numbers, while moisture-loving wild flowers and insects such as dragonflies provide interest in the warmer months.

From Blashford, it is a short distance south on the A338 to return to Ringwood, passing the **Town and Country Experience** museum (See p.50).

© Beaulieu Enterprises Ltd

Beaulieu is one of the most visited places in the New Forest and this chapter features different aspects of the Beaulieu Estate. It also outlines a circuit taking in the eastern borders of the Forest and a number of interesting features on the coastline of Southampton Water and the Solent.

Beaulieu

Beaulieu Village is picturesque, with thatched cottages and the scenic backdrop of the tidal estuary of the Beaulieu River. A group of donkeys frequently strolls down the main street, where several of the Georgian red-brick cottages are tastefully adapted as souvenir shops or tea-rooms. Beaulieu Estate, owned by the Montagu family, is the largest private estate in the Forest. But

*Opposite Page: Palace House, the
home of Lord Montagu, began life as
the gatehouse of Beaulieu Abbey*

to many people, 'Beaulieu' refers not to the village or to the estate but to a major visitor attraction.

Palace House and its grounds form one of the most popular sites in the south of England, with over half a million visitors a year. It all began in 1952, when Lord Montagu opened his family home to the public, one of the first of the stately homes to welcome 'paying guests'.

Vintage and veteran

Today, a single entrance fee covers not only Palace House but also the remains of Beaulieu Abbey and the **National Motor Museum**. No motoring enthusiast will need any recommendation to visit the extensive displays of historic vehicles, ranging from the one-cylinder Knight of 1895 to Formula One cars

of the 1990s.

The Knight was probably the first petrol-driven car to travel on Britain's roads. Its maximum speed was 8mph (13kph) and its builder was fined for not having a traction engine licence or a man to walk in front of his vehicle!

Even those who are not overly fascinated by old vehicles will smile at some of the oddities, like the 1924 Daimler 'Worthington Bottle' or the 1972 Mini 'Outspan Orange'. There are other exhibits with a wide range of appeal, including a complete, and remarkably authentic, 1938 garage with all the tools and all the junk. Full-size shop windows of a similar date include Marks and Spencers, Sainsburys, Burtons and Halfords. 'Wheels' is a Disney-style dark ride, with fascinating scenes from the social history of motoring.

© Beaulieu Enterprises Ltd

National Motor Museum

Beaulieu Abbey

A story concerning the foundation of **Beaulieu Abbey** relates that King John had oppressed a Cistercian community. The king then had a nightmare in which he was being beaten by monks. He decided to make amends for his previous actions by founding a new monastery at Beaulieu in 1204. It was the only religious foundation of his reign, and possessed the largest church of any Cistercian establishment in the kingdom.

The first monks came over from France, hence the spelling of Beaulieu, derived from the original Latin, 'Bellus Locus Regis', the king's beautiful place. (Despite the French origin, the correct pronunciation is 'bew-lee').

Most of the abbey buildings were demolished following the dissolution of the monasteries by Henry VIII. However, two have survived intact. The monks' refectory is now **Beaulieu's parish church** and is usually open to visitors; while the **Domus**, originally the living quarters of the Lay Brothers, houses an informative Exhibition of Monastic Life. The **cloister ruins**, appropriately, are one of the most tranquil spots in the Beaulieu complex.

Palace House

Palace House, as originally built, was the gatehouse of the abbey, though it has been much extended since it passed to an ancestor of Lord Montagu in 1538. Visitors can stroll through the various rooms, where members of staff dressed as a Victorian cook or housekeeper will pass on their knowledge of life 'upstairs and downstairs' in that period.

Between the house and the museum, gardens are laid out in Victorian style. An overhead monorail runs right through the museum building and gives a literal 'overview' of all the facilities. At busy times, a veteran bus transports visitors around the site. Beaulieu lives up to its claim to provide 'a truly eventful day'.

Bucklers Hard

Bucklers Hard, another part of the Estate, is accessible by road or by an attractive riverside walk (2½ miles (4km) south of Beaulieu). It was established in the eighteenth century as a ship-building community. The 'village street' was built 80ft (25m) wide so that whole oak trunks could be rolled down to the slipways on the Beaulieu River.

Bucklers Hard is a very pleasant place to visit, for a stroll down the street and alongside the river. While most of the cottages are private homes, several have been reconstructed internally with displays of life in the 1790s. There is a marked contrast between the somewhat spartan conditions in the 'labourer's cottage' and the relative comfort of the 'shipwright's cottage'.

Scenes of the New Inn are displayed in the actual rooms formerly used as an inn. Labourers, a shipwright, the landlord of the inn, a blacksmith and the Salt Officer (a collector of taxes on salt) are all represented, drinking, playing cards or doing business.

Adjacent to the inn is the **Maritime Museum** with a must-see model showing Bucklers Hard on Friday 3rd June 1803, three days before the launching of the thirty-six-gun *Euryalus*. She was one of three men-o'-war built here

Nelson's oaks

A story tells that Nelson, concerned about the amount of timber needed to replace naval ships, gave his men acorns to plant while on shore leave. Maybe some of the 200 year-old oaks in the Forest today grew from acorns planted by sailors! Nelson could not have known that, by the time his acorns were mature trees, ships would no longer be built of wood.

that took part in the Battle of Trafalgar. A total of fifty-one wooden warships were constructed at Bucklers Hard in the period 1698-1815, mainly using oak grown in the New Forest.

At the bottom of the street, one room of the Master Builder's House is displayed as the office of Henry Adams, who was responsible for building many of the warships. From the nearby jetty, the *Swiftsure* offers regular cruises down the Beaulieu River in the summer season.

Pony Sales

Heading north from Beaulieu on the B3056 Lyndhurst road, after 1 mile (1.5km) there is a T-junction. The right turn leads directly to Ipley Cross by way of some pleasant woodland and heathland scenery, with two car parks as bases to explore this area. Alternatively, the road ahead leads to **Beaulieu Road Station**.

Beside the rail station on the London-Southampton-Bournemouth line is the Beaulieu Hotel. Across the road,

between the railway and a large clump of Scots pines, is a complex of pens and platforms. On five days in the year, in April, August, September, October and November, this deserted spot comes alive with the atmosphere of a country market. Horse-lovers flock here from miles around for the **Beaulieu Road Pony Sales**; commoners gather to see their foals auctioned; traders set up stalls selling everything a rider might need.

A short distance back towards Beaulieu, a minor road leads across an expanse of open heath to meet the alternative route at Ipley Cross. Shortly before this crossroads the road crosses a small bridge over the Beaulieu River. At this point it is a gravel-bedded stream through a narrow band of woodland.

At Ipley Cross, take the road north, which very shortly passes over a cattle grid, marking the Forest perambulation. The next 6½ miles (10km) of the route pass by farmland and woodland which are just outside the Forest proper, though part of the Heritage Area. Just past the Bold Forester pub, the route takes a dog-leg, left and then right.

Otters & owls

A large sign indicates the **New Forest Otter, Owl and Wildlife Conservation Park**. Many of the smaller mammal species of the British countryside, like mice and hedgehogs, live indoors in re-created habitats. A 'twilight barn' is reserved for normally nocturnal creatures, so that visitors may have a chance to see them while they are active.

The various species of otters are always fascinating to watch, as they play in their large pens and pools. The

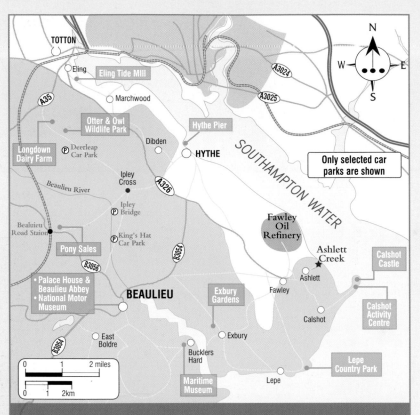

TOTTON
Eling
Eling Tide Mill
Marchwood
A3024
A3025
Otter & Owl Wildlife Park
Hythe Pier
Dibden
HYTHE
SOUTHAMPTON WATER
A35
Longdown Dairy Farm
Deerleap Car Park
Only selected car parks are shown
Ipley Cross
Beaulieu River
A326
Ipley Bridge
Fawley Oil Refinery
Bealieu Road Staion
King's Hat Car Park
B3054
Ashlett Creek
Calshot Castle
Pony Sales
B3056
Ashlett
Fawley
Calshot Activity Centre
• Palace House & Beaulieu Abbey
• National Motor Museum
BEAULIEU
Exbury Gardens
Calshot
B3054
East Boldre
Exbury
Bucklers Hard
Lepe Country Park
0   1   2 miles
0   1   2km
Maritime Museum
Lepe

Beaulieu & The Eastern Borders

Beaulieu Abbey

© Beaulieu Enterprises Ltd

Above: Bucklers Hard

Right: Monorail and bus transporting visitors around the Beaulieu site

Below: Beaulieu Road Pony Sale

enclosures for wild boar, Scottish wild cat, lynx and pine martens, as well as the large owl aviaries, are situated on meandering nature trails within mature woodland. But for many visitors, the most enthralling experience is to enter the deer glade, where sika and other species take little notice of people walking within a very short distance of them.

Fresian cows and friendly rabbits

Only three-quarters of a mile (1km) beyond the Otter and Owl Park is **Longdown Activity Farm**. 100 Fresian cows live here – a commercial dairy herd which is milked daily in a modern computerised parlour.

Longdown, as well as being a busy dairy farm, has many other animals for visitors to see – and for small children to feed and to pet. There are families of remarkably greedy goats, several breeds of sheep and pigs and many types of poultry. The rabbits are in walk-in pens and will happily take food from the hand. Staff organise regular sessions of baby chick handling and bottle-feeding of calves and of lambs, an experience which delights most children (and a lot of adults as well!).

Eling Tide Mill

Just beyond Longdown, take care making a right turn onto the A35 dual carriageway and continue towards Southampton. At the second round-about, turn right onto the A326 Fawley road. After half a mile (0.8km), take a left turn into the delightfully named

Jacob's Gutter Lane, then left again into the village of Eling. There is a car park on the left. A short walk across a narrow bridge (with a toll to pay if you drive over it) takes you to **Eling Tide Mill**.

There has been a mill here, operated by the tide, at least since the Domesday Book. The present Georgian brick building was abandoned in the 1940s and restored in the 1980s. Today it is the only working tide mill in the world, regularly producing stone-ground wholemeal flour as well as crushed oats as feed for New Forest ponies.

At high tide, the sluice gates are closed, trapping sea-water above the mill. As the tide goes out, a considerable height differential develops between the water above and below the mill. The miller opens the gates and water flows under the mill, operating the mill-wheels. By this means, milling is possible for up to eight hours a day, although often at unsociable hours! Unlike a conventional watermill, there is no chance of a shortage of power during a period of drought.

Across the road from the mill is the **Totton and Eling Heritage Centre**, established by the local historical society.

Back across the bridge, Eling village has a remarkably rural aspect, considering how close it is to the urban sprawl of Totton. **St Mary's Church**, though extensively restored in Victorian times, has a fine thirteenth-century chancel arch, as well as features which may remain from the original Saxon church.

South of Eling is a group of communities collectively known as 'the

Waterside'. With the area's modern suburban and industrial development, it is difficult to imagine a time when the New Forest extended to the shore here, but there are still a few thatched cottages in **Marchwood**.

There is a military port here, and a memorial near the parish church commemorates men of the Royal Fleet Auxiliary who lost their lives in the Falklands War.

Hythe

Follow signs to **Hythe**, avoiding the busy A326. This large village has a traffic-free shopping centre with most facilities that visitors might need. Much of the dormitory development here is due to the ease of commuting to Southampton, using a route that visitors may wish to take.

A small electric train, dating from 1917 and the oldest pier train in the world (confirmed by the '*Guinness Book of Records*') carries passengers along the length of **Hythe Pier**. From this point,

Hythe's famous sons

In the 1930s, Hythe was the embarkation point for Imperial Airways' flying-boat services to all parts of the Empire. At around the same time, T E Lawrence, better known as Lawrence of Arabia, lived in the village while he was testing power-boats built here for the RAF. Another famous resident, till his death in 1999, was Sir Christopher Cockerell – Hythe can claim to be the birthplace of the hovercraft.

the **Hythe Ferry** operates a regular service to Town Quay, Southampton, with buses into the city centre. Even if not intending to spend time in Southampton, a half-hour round-trip 'mini cruise'is an excellent way of seeing the shipping in Southampton Water.

Ashlett Creek

From Hythe, follow signs to Fawley. This village has given its name to the largest oil refinery in Europe and to a large oil-fired power station. But just beyond the original village of Fawley is **Ashlett Creek**, a surprisingly peaceful inlet situated between these two great industrial complexes.

The creek is overlooked by yacht club premises, formerly a tide mill, with the Jolly Sailor pub nearby. Opposite, and beyond the public hard, is the start of a footpath leading to Calshot. It follows the sea-wall alongside salt-marshes, with the power station towering overhead on the right.

Calshot

The B3053 leads in 1½ miles (2.5km) to Calshot. Drive through the village to the shore, turn left and follow the promenade to the car park. Beyond this point, **Calshot Spit** is a narrow shingle headland, with **Calshot Castle** at its tip.

In 1539-40, Henry VIII feared invasion, following a treaty between Francis I and the Holy Roman Emperor, Charles V. To counteract the supposed threat, which never materialised, he had a chain of castles constructed along the south coast. Calshot Castle was built in eighteen months using masonry

Otter (above) and Northern Lynx (right) at the New Forest Otter Owl and Wildlife Conservation Park

taken from the demolition of Beaulieu Abbey.

The castle is quite small, roughly circular, with its outer walls high on the landward side but lower where cannon commanded the entrance to Southampton Water. For the modern visitor, it is worth climbing to this position for the superb views. Inside, an exhibition illustrates the history of the castle from 1539 to the present day.

Through two world wars, Calshot was the RAF's flying-boat base. Sir Winston Churchill made his first flight from here. It was the base of the famous Supermarine S6 sea-plane, forerunner of the Spitfire and the outright winner of the Schneider Trophy in 1931. Sunderland flying-boats took part in the 1948 Berlin Air Lift. The giant hangars, an historic survival of an important phase in aviation history, now house **Calshot Activity Centre**, with the S6 commemorated by a shell mosaic on a nearby wall.

Lepe

Head back towards Fawley on the B3053 but take the first minor road to the left, which leads to **Lepe Country Park**. A sand and shingle beach is backed by low cliffs, with views across the Solent to the Isle of Wight. With

Ashlett Creek

Cowes nearly opposite, there are almost invariably yachts on the water. Lepe is a popular spot for wind-surfers and, for the less active, a good place for beach-combing!

A walk east along the shore passes a navigational beacon at Stansore Point. The Isle of Wight is less than 1 mile (1.5km) away, so gas and electricity mains and some telephone cables pass under the Solent here. Beyond the beacon, the walk skirts part of the

Windsurfer at Lepe (Isle of Wight in background)

North Solent National Nature Reserve. Pools in this area, some brackish and some freshwater, attract redshanks, herons, shelduck and other birds.

Near the most westerly of the car parks stand slate-clad coastguard cottages built in the 1850s. Nearby, almost on the foreshore, is the white-painted Watch House, formerly the coastguard lookout station, sited where it had a good view of the mouth of the Beaulieu River. The intertidal area here consists of mud-flats and attracts many wading birds such as oyster-catchers and dunlin.

Exbury Gardens

Leave Lepe by the lane which at first leads westwards along the shore, then head inland to Exbury; just beyond the village is the entrance to **Exbury Gardens**.

These famous gardens, extending to over 200 acres (81 hectares), were first laid out in the 1920s by Lionel de Roth-

Places to Visit

Bucklers Hard

Beaulieu, Brockenhurst, SO42 7XB
☎ 01590 616203
www.bucklershard.co.uk
Maritime Museum; historic eighteenth century village with reconstructed interiors; riverside walks; cafeteria; partial wheelchair access (not Museum); Master Builder's House Hotel with public bars and restaurant. Pay-and-Display car park. Open daily 10am–5pm Mar to Jun, 10am–5.30pm Jul to Aug; 10am–5pm Sept to Oct, 10.30am–4.30pm Nov to Feb. 'Swiftsure' cruises operate from Easter to Oct, times on Pier Kiosk.

Calshot Activity Centre

Calshot Spit, Fawley, Southampton, SO45 1BR
☎ 023 8089 2077
www.calshot.com
One of Britain's largest Outdoor activity centres. Open: daily 08.30am–10pm.

Calshot Castle

English Heritage
Calshot Spit, nr Fawley, SO4 1BR
☎ 023 8089 2023
Sixteenth century coastal castle, with interpretive details and superb views of Southampton Water and Solent. Parking and disabled access. Open daily 10am–4.30pm Apr to Sept.

Eling Tide Mill

Eling Lane, Totton
☎ 023 8086 9575
Working tide mill; partial wheelchair access; displays; shop selling stone-ground flour and gifts. Open: all year 10am–4pm Wed to Sun (plus Bank Holiday Mondays; not Christmas Day and Boxing Day). Milling depends on tide – phone for times.

Exbury Gardens & Steam Railway

Exbury, SO45 1AZ
(signed from B3054 east of Beaulieu)
☎ 023 8089 1203
www.exbury.co.uk
Gardens specialising in rhododendrons, camellias and azaleas; picnic area; miniature steam railway; tea-room; restaurant; gift shop; plant centre; partial wheelchair access; special events through the year. Open: 10am–5pm, Mar to early Nov.

Lepe Country Park

Lepe, Exbury SO45 1AD
☎ 023 8089 9108
Three large Pay-and-Display seashore car parks; beach with dog-free and dog-welcome areas; shore walks; information centre and gift shop; licensed restaurant; refreshment kiosk; picnic areas; barbecue (bookable); children's play area; toilets (including

schild. They are undoubtedly one of the finest woodland gardens to be seen in the country. Exbury is magnificent in early summer with extensive displays of Magnolias, azaleas, rhododendrons and camellias.

However, this should not be taken to imply that the gardens are not worth visiting at other times of the year. The daffodil meadow provides colour in early spring, while the changing tints of many of the trees make an autumn visit worthwhile. In high summer, the rose garden is at its best. A series of disabled). Open daily 7.30am until dusk (up to 9pm in Aug). Park office open daily in summer, weekends only in winter. Ranger on site at all times.

Longdown Activity Farm

Longdown, near Ashurst, SO40 7EH
☎ 023 8029 2837
www.longdownfarm.co.uk
Working dairy farm, milking viewed from gallery from 2.30pm; friendly farm animals for children to hold and feed; gift shop; refreshment kiosk; picnic and play area; disabled access most areas. Open: daily 10am–5pm, early Feb to end-Oct and weekends up till Christmas.

National Motor Museum, Palace House & Beaulieu Abbey

SO42 7ZN
☎ 01590 612345 (24 hours)
www.beaulieu.co.uk

Displays on aspects of motoring history including 'Wheels' dark ride; gardens; picnic areas, monorail; various rides and simulators; Palace House (guided tours are bookable – additional charge); Abbey ruins; Food Court for drinks, snacks and meals; wheelchair access to most parts. Many special events throughout the year. Open: daily from 10am–6pm (5pm Oct to May) throughout the year, except Christmas Day.

The New Forest Otter, Owl & Wildlife Conservation Park

Longdown, nr Ashurst, SO40 4UH
☎ 023 8029 2408
www.ottersandowls.co.uk

Many species of otters, owls, deer, wild boar, etc in enclosures set in 25 acres (10 hectares) of woodland; full wheelchair access; free parking; shop with wildlife related gifts; tea-room. Open daily, summer 10am–5.30pm; winter 10am–dusk.

Totton & Eling Heritage Centre

Eling Lane, Totton
☎ 023 8066 6339

Tableaux and displays on the history of the area; temporary exhibitions; wheelchair access; café. Open: Wed to Sun 10am–4.30pm in summer, 10.30am –4pm in winter.

small ponds adds reflections to Exbury's beauty.

Turn left on leaving the gardens and continue along this road till you reach a double junction at the Royal Oak pub; turn left and left again. The B3054 returns you to Beaulieu.

Requiem for a Wren

In 1942, Exbury House was taken over by the Royal Navy, and later became known as *HMS Mastodon*. In the run-up to D-Day, there were marines camped in the grounds and large numbers of Wrens were billeted in cottages in Exbury and Beaulieu. The Beaulieu River swarmed with landing craft, some too large for easy manoeuvrability in the narrow estuary. A large part of Nevil Shute's novel *'Requiem for a Wren'* is set in *HMS Mastodon* and in most respects his account is historically accurate.

Exbury Gardens and Exbury engine Mariloo at American Garden

Three ponies grazing on Penn Common, Bramshaw

The north-eastern part of the Forest includes several commons managed by the National Trust. Not far away, south of the village of Brook, is the Rufus Stone, believed to mark the spot where King William II was killed.

Bramshaw Commons

The **Bramshaw Commons** are distinguished on the Ordnance Survey map by the 'NT' symbol. They include seven named commons, as well as several smaller greens and most of the roadside verges around the village of Bramshaw.

Before 1964, when they were first brought within the perambulation, their position was anomalous. Villagers had grazing rights on their local commons,

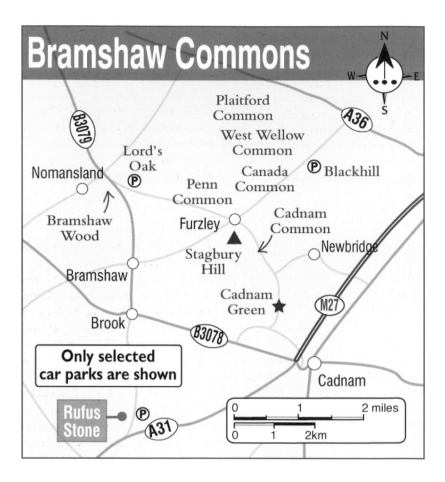

Bramshaw Commons

Plaitford Common
West Wellow Common
Lord's Oak
Nomansland
Canada Common
Ⓟ Blackhill
Penn Common
Bramshaw Wood
Furzley
Cadnam Common
Stagbury Hill
Newbridge
Bramshaw
Cadnam Green
Brook
Only selected car parks are shown
Cadnam
Rufus Stone

0   1   2 miles
0   1   2km

---

without charge. There were no fences, so their livestock could and did wander into the Forest proper, whose commoners pay a fee for each depastured animal. This also resulted in animal health problems.

Today the Verderers and Agisters have the same responsibilities on these 'adjacent commons' as elsewhere. The National Trust, however, is the landowner, so the Forestry Commission has no powers in the area. The commons in the west of the Forest, near Ibsley, have a similar recent history and present status.

Touring the commons

The commons may be explored on the following circular route from Cadnam, but there are several other interesting narrow lanes and byways, some of which will be mentioned in passing.

Just east of M27 junction 1 is the original 'Cadnam Roundabout', one of the earliest roundabouts in the area and an important crossroads for centuries. Nearby is the historic thatched inn, the Sir John Barleycorn. Take the A31 northward, signposted Romsey, for three-quarters of a mile (1.2km), then

Managing the heathland

The landscape around Blackhill is varied, with stands of Scots pine and of silver birch adjacent to the heathland. A few rhododendron bushes are very attractive in early summer. However, all three species, pine, birch and especially rhododendron, invade and ultimately take over heathland if left to their own devices. Under the partially EU-funded LIFE project, the National Trust has been working to reduce this invasion.

turn left onto a minor road signposted Newbridge. This passes under the motorway and, just after Newbridge village, enters the Forest at **Cadnam Common**.

Just after the cattle grid, Cadnam Lane leads off to the left; it is almost indistinguishable from the New Forest boundary on the OS Outdoor Leisure map. A detour down this lane leads to **Cadnam Green**, small but generally popular with grazing animals.

Continuing ahead, Furzley Road meanders over Cadnam Common, an area of short grass with gorse bushes, some marshy areas and some unfenced woodland. Just before the minor cross-roads at **Furzley**, a mound on the left is known as **Stagbury Hill**. Climb to the top, where an old OS triangulation pillar stands near a Bronze Age burial mound or tumulus, for good views over the common lands.

A detour to the right at this cross-roads leads, after 1 mile (1.5km), to

Blackhill car park. Elsewhere, it is usually possible to find an informal lay-by, and the National Trust has not made its land quite so strictly 'car-free' as Forestry Commission land. Drivers should still remember that parking on grassland damages grazing and is to be avoided.

Penn Common

Returning from Blackhill to Furzley crossroad, the road to the right leads to **Penn Common**. Mixed herds of ponies, donkeys and cattle are often to be seen here, grazing on the close-cropped turf and sometimes on the dense areas of gorse bushes. Sheep may also be encountered in this area and, mainly in the autumn, pigs may be actively 'rooting' in the soft grass-land, leaving small 'ploughed-up' areas behind them.

If walking on Penn Common, there are two spots where tracks lead, between enclosed fields on either side, through to the greater expanse of **Plaitford, West Wellow** and **Canada Commons**. A car park here, provided by Wellow Parish Council, may be reached from the main A36 road by taking the turning signposted Canada. The unusual name seems to derive from the fact that this Forest-edge settlement was being 'newly colonised' at a time when a much greater new colony was in the news.

The road alongside Penn Common continues through farmland and A&O Woods to **Lord's Oak car park**, a good centre for exploring **Bramshaw Wood**. The mature oak and beech trees are a wonderful sight, especially in the autumn as the leaves turn colour. In the

Furzley Common in snow, from Stagsbury Hill

The Right of Common Pasture of Sheep is little practised nowadays but they may sometimes be seen among the gorse bushes on the Bramshaw Commons

thirteenth century, some of the timber used in the construction of Salisbury Cathedral came from this wood.

Nomansland & Bramshaw

Shortly after this car park, there is a T-junction with the B3079 road. A detour may be made here to **Nomansland** – right at the junction and then the next left. The village has the cottages on one side of the road (in Wiltshire and outside the perambulation) and the cricket pitch on a Forest lawn on the other side (in Hampshire and in the Forest). It used to be 'no-man's-land' as the Forest keepers had no jurisdiction over those who lived outside the boundary.

Back at the T-junction, continue southwards on the B3079 and through the scattered village of **Bramshaw**. Near the crossroads known as Stock's Cross, there is a small green, a favourite haunt of pigs. The road to the left leads back to Furzley; a stretch of hedgebank here is a mass of foxgloves in the summer.

The B3079 passes Bramshaw's village post office and general store; also a small petrol station. Immediately after the junction with the B3078 and just before the Bell Inn and the Green Dragon, there is a right turn signposted 'Rufus Stone via Ford'.

However, the **Green Dragon** in **Brook** is well worth a mention. It is a thatched inn, set back a little from the road; ponies often stand around its forecourt in the summer. The interior has been extended and brought up to modern standards, but still retains some

features of its days as a small commoners' 'local'. Of these, the most interesting are 'bends' of leather mounted on the wall, each with a selection of the brand marks used by commoners on their livestock.

The Rufus Stone

The lane to the Rufus Stone is narrow and twisting, with small hedged fields on either side. The ford is often dry, but motorists may need to drive through a few inches of water after wet weather. At the hamlet of Upper Canterton, the well-known public house, the **Sir Walter Tyrell**, looks out onto a large Forest lawn, part of Castle Malwood Walk. A short distance on through the woods is the **Rufus Stone**, with a car park opposite.

This is said to be the most visited spot in the New Forest, despite the fact that the 'Stone' (actually a three-sided metal pillar) can be read and admired in a very short time. However, the memorial is a reminder of the most famous of New Forest tales (see box on p.80).

If not following the itinerary in this chapter, motorists can approach the Rufus Stone from the A31. The right turn off the west-bound side involves the dangerous manoeuvre of crossing the fast east-bound carriageway and is strongly advised against. Turning left off the east-bound carriageway is, of course, no problem.

On leaving Rufus Stone, cyclists should return to Cadnam via Brook. Motorists may filter onto the A31 east-bound, turn right at M27 Junction 1, then follow the A31 a short distance back to the starting point at Cadnam.

The Death of William Rufus

The son of William the Conqueror, King William II, was commonly known as William Rufus because of his florid complexion and red hair. On 2nd August 1100, he was hunting in the New Forest with his younger brother Henry and a group of nobles. An arrow, carelessly aimed by Sir Walter Tyrell, hit the king and killed him outright. The king was taken for burial in Winchester. Henry was crowned on the 5th of the same month.

This is the full story, as far as any reasonably contemporary accounts go, but the tale has been embroidered in subsequent centuries and has acquired the status of legend. It is hardly surprising that several conspiracy theories have emerged.

Late in the day, it was said, Rufus had shot an arrow at a stag and wounded it. Tyrell shot another arrow which glanced off an oak tree before hitting the king. Fearing the consequences, he immediately fled to France, having a blacksmith reverse his horse's shoes to confuse any pursuers – there were none. The spot where he forded the River Avon is still known as Avon Tyrell.

Henry, realising that the throne might well pass to his other brother, Duke Robert of Normandy, made indecent haste to Winchester to claim the treasury and on to Westminster to have himself crowned king. A few months later, he married Edyth, to whom Rufus had previously paid court only to be refused by her aunt, the Abbess of Romsey. As Edyth

The Rufus Stone

was a Scottish princess descended from the Saxon kings of England, this was a good dynastic marriage for a Norman king. Thus, Henry seems to have had motives for arranging his brother's elimination. This is supported by his later pardoning of Tyrell and allowing him to return to England.

On the day of the fateful hunt, the other two nobles in the party also abandoned the king's body. William of Breteuil left to proclaim the right of Duke Robert to the throne, while Robert Fitz Hamon departed for no apparent reason. It was left to a charcoal burner by the name of Purkiss to transport

The Inn sign shows the death of William Rufus

the corpse to Winchester on his cart. William was buried in the cathedral, directly under the tower. When the tower collapsed seven years later, many blamed the presence of an evil king's body beneath it.

William II, an unpopular king and something of a heretic, had always been disliked by the Church. A month before the king's death, the Abbott of Shrewsbury had preached a sermon of veiled criticism which included the words "the arrow swift to wound is already drawn out of the quiver. Soon will the blow be struck". So perhaps the Church was involved in a conspiracy.

The earliest written statement of where, exactly, in the New Forest the death occurred was made over 400 years after the event. Some historians believe that a spot near Beaulieu was meant. However, a commemorative stone was erected in Canterton Glen in 1745, because, it was said, the original oak from which the arrow had glanced, had fallen. Following damage to the stone, the present cast-iron pillar was placed over it. Yet the metal pillar is hollow – there is no actual 'Rufus stone', a final twist to this enduring mystery.

The market town and ancient seaport of Lymington possesses much to recommend it to the visitor. Along the coastline to the west are the small seaside resorts of Milford-on-Sea, Barton-on-Sea and Highcliffe, as well as the town of New Milton. While none of these settlements is within the perambulation, the area has always had close links with the Forest.

Lymington

The history of the area 'between the New Forest and the Solent' is very effectively displayed in the **St Barbe Museum**. It showcases the importance of the sea and of the marshes in the economy of the area over the centuries. According to Daniel Defoe in 1720, smuggling was the main commercial activity of Lymington. The production of sea-salt by evaporation was, for centuries, the most important (legal) local occupation, reaching its peak of production in the 1770s. Farming, local industries including boat-building, and the beginnings of sea-bathing are all represented. The Gallery houses temporary exhibitions of fine art, crafts, local history and photography.

Lymington has a long and broad High Street, running down from

St Barbe Art Gallery

the imposing tower and cupola of St Thomas's Church, almost to the river. On Saturdays, traffic must defer to the market as large numbers of stalls, selling a very wide variety of goods, occupy both sides of the street.

The Quay

At the bottom of the High Street is **Quay Hill**, traffic-free, steep and cobbled. With its Georgian houses and bay windows, it is no doubt one of the most photographed street scenes in Hampshire. A short walk, around the bend at the bottom, along the much narrower Quay Street, with tea-rooms and specialist shops, brings the visitor out onto the **Quay** itself. There is a small fishing fleet based here, with chandlers nearby for the many yachts that fill the marinas of Lymington River estuary.

Puffin Cruises offers short trips through the western Solent, with fine views of Hurst Castle and The Needles, and provides a foot passenger service to the **Isle of Wight**. The vehicle ferry to the island, operated by **Wightlink**, has a terminal on the other side of the river. There is, of course, a great deal to see on the Isle of Wight, which is the subject of another Landmark Visitors Guide.

At the far end of Bath Road from the Quay are the premises of Lymington Town Sailing Club, situated in the eighteenth-century Bath House. Alongside is a rare survival nowadays, an open-air swimming pool, open May to August. A footpath starting nearby follows the sea-wall 5 miles (8km) or so to Keyhaven and continues along the shingle spit to Hurst Castle.

Sea Aster & Brent Geese

The coastline from the mouth of the Lymington River to the spit forms part of the **Lymington** and **Keyhaven Nature Reserves**. The area inside the sea-wall is used as grazing land, while on the seaward side there are tidal salt-marshes and mud-flats. It is here that salt water was once allowed to settle in lagoons called salterns for initial evaporation, before being boiled to extract the salt.

The nature reserves have a great deal of biological interest, with salt-loving wild flowers such as the sea aster and golden samphire, and abundant birdlife. Over 3,000 Brent geese winter in the area and form a spectacular sight when a great flock swoops in to settle on one of the grazing marshes. Large numbers of terns and gulls, of a variety of species, nest in the reserves.

If you cycle or drive from Lymington to Keyhaven, turn left onto the B3058, then left again into Lymore Lane. **Braxton Gardens** are centred around the courtyard of a Victorian farmstead, with a herb garden, a farm shop in one of the barns and formal planting in the old walled garden. The narrow lane leads to Keyhaven; alternatively use the B3058.

Hurst Castle

Keyhaven is a small village with a pub, a boatyard and a marina. It is another 2½ miles (3.5km) from here to Hurst Castle, and much of this is quite hard walking on the shingle bank. There is a small amount of parking in Saltgrass Lane, the nearest point to the castle

– and a favourite haunt of bird-watchers, especially in the winter months. In addition, a small ferry-boat operates between Keyhaven and the castle; a good compromise is to walk one way and take the ferry in the other direction. (The ferry also offers Solent cruises and trips to the Isle of Wight.)

Hurst Castle, like that at Calshot, originated as one of Henry VIII's chain of coastal fortresses, but it was greatly enlarged in the 1860s. Situated only three quarters of a mile (1.2km) from the nearest point on the Isle of Wight, this was an ideal spot to defend the entrance to the Solent. The castle was manned and in continuous military use from Tudor times till World War II; guns from most periods are on display. Charles I was imprisoned here before his trial and beheading. There are two lighthouses on the spit near the castle.

To the west of Keyhaven is the small seaside resort of **Milford-on-Sea**, with a shingle beach on Christchurch Bay. A little way back from the sea, adjacent to the High Street and near the thirteenth-century parish church, is a traditional village green – scene of a pitched battle between smugglers and militia in the eighteenth century. The green is still used for Maypole Dancing and for the August Bank Holiday carnival.

Motorbikes & Earthworks

From Milford, the B3058 leads to New Milton, but a slight detour will take in the little resort of **Barton-on-Sea**. The cliffs here are composed of fossil-containing sands and clays, and are constantly being eroded by landslips.

There were only fifteen cottages in Barton before 1870 – and six of these were reserved for coastguards. It is now continuous with the bustling town of **New Milton**, which also consisted of only a few cottages and a church until the railway arrived in 1888. Its most conspicuous building is a massive, castellated, red-brick water tower! The **Forest Arts Centre** in Old Milton Road stages amateur and professional theatre, music and dance, with workshops, arts and crafts and a gallery.

Leave New Milton on the B3058. At a crossroads, the B3055 leads left to the **Sammy Miller Motorcycle Museum**, housed in the former farm buildings of Bashley Manor. Extensive glass cases hold many hundreds of trophies from British and European championships, won by Sammy in motorcycle trials, road-racing and other events. Well over 200 gleaming motorcycles are on display, some of them going back to the early years of the twentieth century; most are in full working order.

At the same crossroads, the right turn on the B3055 leads to **Tiptoe Church**. At the church, turn right to Hordle, then left at the Three Bells pub.

Follow this lane for about 3 miles (5km) to **Buckland Rings**. There are footpaths leading to the tree-covered earthworks of this Iron Age fort which has three ramparts and two ditches enclosing an area of about 11 acres (4.5 hectares).

Woodland Garden

A 1-mile (1.6km) detour north from here leads to **Spinners Garden** (see p.87), which is found down a twisting

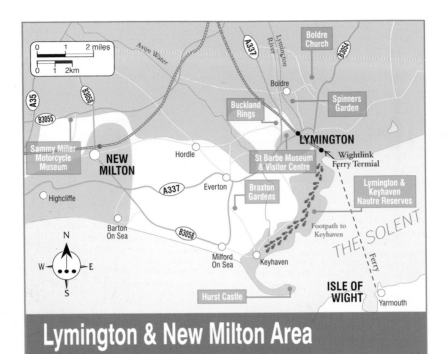

Lymington & New Milton Area

Above: Quay Hill, Lymington

Left: Bagging the 'catch' of oysters, Lymington Quay

Below: Sammy Miller Motorcycle Museum. The foreground shows a 1962 Triumph 350cc model

The Quay, Lymington

Spinners Garden

Boldre Church

lane at Boldre, signposted from the A337. The owners bought a 3-acre (1.2-hectare) plot, already partly-wooded, in 1961. Over the next twenty years, working only in spare time at first, they gradually developed it into a sloping woodland garden.

In the highest part of the garden, rhododendrons and azaleas predominate; lower down, there are boggy areas, home to royal ferns, iris and candelabra primulas. Japanese maples provide a mass of autumn colour, while a variety of bulbs flower under the trees in spring. A national collection of trilliums is maintained here.

Boldre is a scattered village in the valley of the Lymington River. **St John the Baptist Church**, reached around narrow twisting lanes, stands on a ridge some distance from most of the houses. It contains a memorial to William Gilpin, author of *Remarks on Forest Scenery*, which extolled the picturesque nature of the New Forest. When he became vicar here in 1777, Boldre was known as a lawless area, but he worked to improve the lot of the parishioners, providing a school and a poorhouse.

From Boldre, it is less than 3 miles (5km) back to the centre of Lymington.

'Through this picturesque country I have led my reader geographically; and have presented him with a great variety of beautiful scenes – woods – lawns – heaths – forest-distances and sea-coast views. I have adorned these scenes with their proper appendages, wild horses, deer and other picturesque inhabitants.'

Remarks on Forest Scenery by William Gilpin (Vicar of Boldre) 1791

Places to Visit

St Barbe Museum & Art Gallery

New Street, Lymington, SO41 9BH
☎ 01590 676969
www.stbarbe-museum.org.uk
Displays on history of the area between the New Forest and the Solent; temporary exhibitions; full disabled access. Open: 10am–4pm all year Mon to Sat (last entry 3.30pm).

Sammy Miller Motorcycle Museum

Bashley Cross Rd, New Milton, BH25 5SZ
(on B3055, signposted from A35)
☎ 01425 620777
http://museum.sammymiller.co.uk
One of the world's largest motorcycle museums; partial wheelchair access; tea-room; craft shops and gypsy caravan are sited in the same courtyard. Open daily 10am–4.30pm. Closed Dec and Jan.

Lymington and Keyhaven Nature Reserves

Access from Keyhaven or from Normandy Lane, Lymington
☎ 01489 774400
www.hwt.org.uk
View from footpath on sea-wall. Information leaflet from Hampshire Wildlife Trust. Open at all times.

Hurst Castle

On foot along the shingle spit or by ferry from Keyhaven
☎ 01590 642500 to check ferry times
☎ 01590 642500 (Office)
☎ 01590 642344 (Castle)

www.hurstcastle.co.uk
Good views of Isle of Wight and of Solent shipping; tea-room. Open: daily 10.30am–5.30pm (4pm in Oct) Apr to Oct. Nov to Mar Weekends only 10.30am–4pm

Spinners Garden

School Lane, Boldre, SO41 5QE
☎ 01590 673347
www.spinnersgarden.co.uk
Woodland garden overlooking the valley of the Lymington River; very wide range of hardy rare plants on sale in nursery; tours by appointment; no dogs. Open: 10am–5pm Mon to Sat; garden only fully open. Apr to mid-Sept. Free admission to nursery at all times.

Braxton Gardens

Lymore Lane, Milford on Sea
Knot garden; plant centre; farm shop; fishing at Everton Grange Lake. Open: daily 9.30am–5pm Mon to Sat; 10am–4pm Sun.

Buckland Rings

Near junction of A377 and B3054, north of Lymington
☎ 01962 846120
Iron Age hill-fort; permissive footpaths provided by Hampshire Countryside Service. Only nearby parking is provided for patrons of the Tollhouse Inn; walk back along the Hordle Road – take care, no footway for 50 yards.

While there is more than sufficient to occupy visitors' time within the immediate area of the New Forest, it is appreciated that holiday-makers may wish to take day trips to other places of interest. Having devoted most of this book to countryside matters, here we concentrate on some of the historic towns and cities and a few major attractions. Most can be reached by public transport, but the boxes give directions by road from Lyndhurst; all are within an hour's journey time by car.

Romsey

Romsey's main interest is in its **Abbey** church, one of the finest pieces of Norman architecture in England. The abbey was founded in about 907AD and Edyth was a novice here – the Scottish/Saxon princess who was prevented from marrying William Rufus by the Abbess (her aunt) but who then became Henry I's Queen Matilda – *see* Rufus Stone.

The present building was commenced in 1120, two years after Matilda's death, and it may be that Henry partially financed it in memory of his queen. After the Dissolution, most of the abbey was demolished, but the church was bought by the town in 1544 and has been its parish church ever since. It has many features of interest to the visitor, including the original 'sale document' with Henry VIII's seal.

Not far from the abbey is **King John's House**, a thirteenth-century stone house with a later timber-framed extension and many fascinating features,

> ## Romsey
>
> Take A337 from Lyndhurst to Junction 1 M27, leave at Junction 2, then A31 to Romsey. 11 miles (17.5km)
> More details from Romsey TIC:
> ☎ 01794 512987

including graffiti leftby Edward I's courtiers in February 1306. A linked **Heritage Centre** has interesting displays.

The town has a bigger proportion of independent shops than many towns – a pleasant place to browse. The Market Place centres on a statue of Lord Palmerston, the Victorian prime minister who lived at **Broadlands House**. This is now the home of Lord Brabourne, the grandson of Earl Mountbatten. A visit to the house includes a major exhibition about the life of the Earl.

Mottisfont Abbey is a National Trust property, a few miles north of Romsey. The gardens stay open late into the evening at the height of the rose season, when they are particularly spectacular.

Paultons Park

Four miles (6.4km) from Romsey is **Paultons Park**, which provides interest for every member of the family. Originally it was the park of a country house, which burnt down in 1963, and the many separate rides and attractions are set in spacious park surroundings. Those of historic bent will enjoy the museum of Romany life, with life-sized displays and many colourful and genuine gypsy caravans.

For the animal-lover, there are deer and llama paddocks, 250 species of exotic birds in spacious aviaries, 40 species of wildfowl living free on the lake – and several species of dinosaurs! These full size models are brilliantly displayed in a wooded swamp and viewed from a boardwalk.

For children there is the extensive Kids' Kingdom adventure playground for the over-fives and a Tiny Tots' Town for smaller children. The rides range from the gentle Rabbit Ride to the Raging River log flume, which is not for the faint-hearted! For those wanting a more tranquil day out, the gardens, aviaries and river walk are well separated from the livelier activities.

Moors Valley Country Park

Moors Valley, while beyond the Forest, is a largely wooded area also administered by the Forestry Commission (with East Dorset Council). It is a wonderful day out, with something to interest children of all ages. Also, it's free apart from car parking.

A Visitor Centre houses a café, gift shop and a cycle hire centre. Nearby there is an excellent adventure playground for the older children, with gentler facilities for the younger ones. There is a large picnic area and a narrow-gauge steam railway (additional charge).

Way-marked routes for walkers and for cyclists lead around a lake and through the woods; the longer walks take you away from the crowds. One trail leads high into the tree-tops, but the most popular is the Play Trail (¾ mile, 1.2km) with large wooden play structures at intervals.

For the really adventurous, Go Ape is a series of commando-style aerial walks and zip-wire slides.

Paultons Park

Ower, nr. Romsey, SO51 6AL (short distance from Exit 2 of M27)
☎ 023 8081 4442
www.paultonspark.co.uk
Over 50 rides and attractions including: exotic birds; historical exhibits; full wheelchair access; restaurants; picnic areas; mothers' room; shops.
Open: daily 10am–6.30pm (last entry 4.30pm) mid-Mar–Oct; weekends only Nov–Christmas; earlier closing spring, autumn and winter.

Moors Valley Country Park

☎ 01425 470721
www.moors-valley.co.uk
A337 to Cadnam, A31 to just beyond Ringwood, leave A31 on slip-road and take third exit on major roundabout, minor road with brown sign for Moors Valley. 20 miles (32km).

No entry fee; parking charges vary by time of day and through the year; can be expensive and busy in school holidays.

Go Ape - no under-10s, safety gear and training provided, charged and pre-bookable. www.goape.co.uk

Southampton

Take A337 to Cadnam, M27 to Junction 3, M271, then Millbrook Road dual carriageway to city centre. Or take A35 via Totton to Millbrook Road. Alternatively, use the ferry from Hythe to Southampton Town Quay. 14 miles (22km) by road. Southampton TIC:
☎ 023 8022 1106.

Southampton

Southampton is a major shopping centre for the whole region, but also has much historic interest. About half of the medieval walls are intact, with thirteen of the original twenty-nine towers still standing. **God's House Tower** houses an archaeological museum; the city also boasts a **Maritime Museum**, a **Hall of Aviation**, a **Medieval Merchant's House** and **Tudor House Museum**.

The magnificent landward gate of the town, the **Bargate**, still stands, as does the **Westgate**, scene of the departure of Henry V's troops before Agincourt and of the Pilgrim Fathers.

The city has many fine parks, including the extensive **Southampton Common**, used for several open-air events in the summer. Parts of the former docks, from which the *Titanic* departed

in 1912, are now developed with restaurants, shops and cinemas.

The Mayflower, the Nuffield Theatre and several smaller venues present a wide variety of drama productions, opera, ballet, concerts and so on. Southampton's **Art Gallery** is housed in the 1930s Civic Centre; a whole room is permanently devoted to Burne-Jones's pre-Raphaelite re-working of the legend of Perseus.

Winchester

Winchester's pedestrianised High Street is on the same alignment as the main street of the Roman town, Venta Belgarum. Winchester was the capital of the Saxon kings of Wessex, the most famous of whom was Alfred the Great. Today, his statue dominates The Broadway. Alfred's grandson became the first king of all England – and Winchester remained the capital.

In Norman times, a great new cathedral was built, only to be largely remodelled in the Perpendicular style of architecture in the fourteenth century. Amongst **Winchester Cathedral**'s many features of interest are the longest nave in

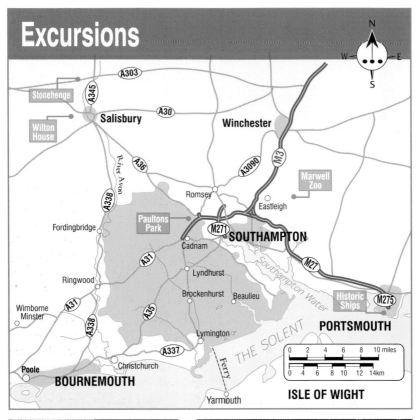

Excursions

Winchester Cathedral

Edge, a new ride at Paultons Park

Europe, the tomb of Jane Austen and the Winchester Bible, beautifully illuminated by twelfth-century monks.

The **Great Hall**, all that is left of Winchester's medieval castle, contains **'King Arthur's Round Table'**. It actually dates from around 1280, with the painted decoration probably added in the reign of Henry VIII.

Other historic buildings include **Wolvesey Castle**; the **Westgate**; the excellent **City Museum** and a collection of no less than five **Military Museums**. Some of the buildings of **Winchester College** date from its foundation in 1382. The College houses the original painting of the *Trusty Servant*, which inspired the name of the pub in Minstead (see p.29).

St Cross Hospital, with its chapel and almshouses, ranks as Britain's oldest charitable institution. It may be reached by a pleasant riverside walk along the Itchen and through the water-meadows. In Winchester, the countryside is never far away and the city contains several

Winchester city mill

Ring tailed Lemur at Marwell Zoo

Winchester

Marwell Wildlife

green spaces, including the tranquil close around the Cathedral. The poet John Keats wrote that Winchester was *'the pleasantest town I was ever in'*.

Today, the city has a modern shopping centre, with small shops in narrow alleys as well as the big stores in the High Street and Brooks Centre. There is a cinema, several theatres, a leisure centre, galleries and a market four days a week. There are also special events through the year including the famous Hat Fair in July. The fair is one of the largest street theatre events anywhere, with buskers and entertainers of all sorts placing their hats on the ground in the hope of contributions.

Marwell Wildlife

Marwell Zoo is situated in open countryside to the south-east of Winchester. Its primary role is conservation and it has an excellent record in the breeding of endangered species. Thus the visitor, while enjoying a fascinating day out, is also making a valuable contribution to the preservation of wildlife.

Siberian tiger and snow leopard, scimitar-horned oryx and Asiatic wild ass, white rhinoceros and pygmy hippopotamus, giraffe and Bactrian camel,

meerkats, ring-tailed coatis and many more species are found at Marwell. Each species has a spacious enclosure providing a habitat as similar to its natural environment as possible.

One of Marwell's success stories is the breeding of Przewalski's wild horse, a native of Mongolia, already extinct in the wild. Closer to home and behind the scenes, Marwell has been active in breeding two of the rarer species found in the New Forest, the sand lizard and the natterjack toad.

Salisbury

The construction of **Salisbury Cathedral** was begun in 1220 and completed within thirty-eight years, though the soaring spire, the tallest in England, was added a generation or two later. The unsurpassed beauty of the building is due, in no small part, to the resulting unity of architectural style. The Chapter House houses one of the four surviving copies of Magna Carta.

1220 was also the date of the foundation of the city, which has retained its original street-plan. Many medieval buildings remain; thanks to water-courses incorporated into the planned street layout, the city avoided the extensive fire damage which devastated so many towns. Part of a present-day shop in Queen Street originated as a house built in 1306, the earliest certainly known date.

Several of the historic houses in the walled **Cathedral Close** may be visited, although most are private homes. **Mompesson House** (used in the filming of *Sense and Sensibility*) was built in 1701, a perfect example of a Queen Anne town house. **The Wardrobe**, so called as it was the bishops' clothing store, is now a regimental museum. The **Salisbury and South Wiltshire Museum** houses several displays of national importance, including the Stonehenge gallery.

Salisbury's large **Market Place** fills with stalls every Tuesday and Saturday, with some spilling out around the ancient **Poultry Cross**. The market has operated continuously since 1361 and is only interrupted on the third Tuesday in October each year, the date of the Charter Fair. During this three-day event, the ancient houses and inns around the Market Place are incongruously dominated by the Big Wheel and other fair-ground attractions.

Salisbury

A337 to Cadnam, then B3079 via Bramshaw to the A36. (Or M27 to Junction 2, onto the A36.). 21 miles (33.5km).
Salisbury TIC:
☎ 01722 334956.

Salisbury has plenty of modern shopping facilities, both big-name stores and local specialist shops. The **Playhouse theatre** is widely admired, attracting a clientele from a wide area, and there are three other venues for theatre, dance, concerts and the like. The Odeon cinema is a listed building – its foyer is a restored fifteenth-century banqueting hall! The annual Salisbury Festival, generally held in May/June, is a major date in the arts calendar.

To the north of the city are the earth-works and ruins of **Old Sarum**, the forerunner of the thirteenth-century city. North again (though somewhat more than an hour's drive from Lynd-hurst) is the World Heritage Site of **Stonehenge**. To the west is **Wilton House**, the stately home of the Earl of Pembroke, which has featured in many films and television productions.

Portsmouth Historic Dockyard

Visitors to the New Forest, especially those interested by the Maritime Museum at Bucklers Hard, may wish to make the trip to Portsmouth to see Nelson's flagship, *HMS Victory*, and other historic ships.

The oldest ship here is the *Mary Rose*, which sank in full view of Henry VIII in 1545, with the loss of around 700 men. The remains of the ship were famously raised in 1982. Today the wreck is still under-going conservation work and may be viewed in a special Ship Hall. Nearby the *Mary Rose Museum* tells a detailed story of life in the Tudor navy.

The *Victory* is the oldest warship in

the world which is still technically in commission. Guided tours include the spot where Admiral Horatio Nelson died within hours of his victory at the Battle of Trafalgar in 1805.

HMS Warrior was revolutionary when she was built in 1860, the first battleship to be constructed of iron rather than wood, and with steam power as well as sail. Her derelict hull was rescued and restored in the 1980s and is equipped just as she was when 700 men lived and worked on her. The captain and officers had relatively luxurious apartments, while the ordinary sailors lived in cramped conditions on the gun decks.

In addition to the three ships, the **Royal Naval Museum** and the **Dockyard Apprentice** exhibition are included in the overall admission charge to the Historic Dockyard.

Portsmouth Historic Ships

Victory Gate, HM Naval Base, PO1 3LJ

A337 to Cadnam, M27 to Junction 12, M275 into Portsmouth city, then follow brown signs to Historic Ships, 34 miles (54.5km).

Portsmouth TIC ☎ 023 9282 6722.

Historic Dockyard ☎ 023 9286 1512 (24 hour information line).

www.historicdockyard.co.uk

HMS Victory

Open from 10am daily all year, except Christmas Eve, Christmas Day and Boxing Day. Dockyard gates close at 6.00pm (Apr-Oct) or 5.30pm (Nov-Mar). However, please note that the closing times of individual attractions within the Historic Dockyard are variable and may be a little earlier than these times.

Left: Dressing up at the Mary Rose
Left bottom: Harbour tours
Below: A fun day for all the family

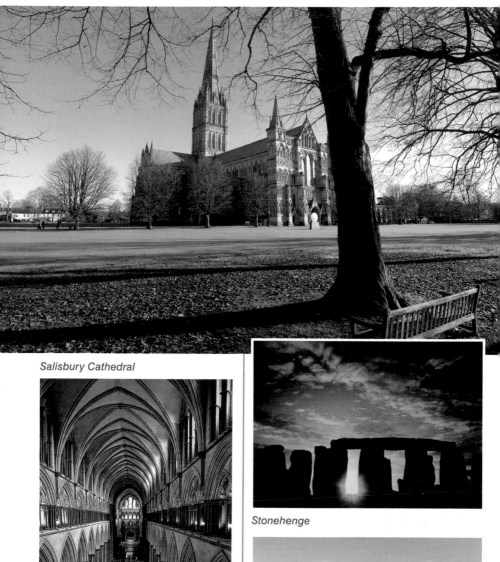

Salisbury Cathedral

The interior of Salisbury Cathedral

Stonehenge

Bournemouth Pier

Bournemouth

Bournemouth possesses everything that one might expect from a major south coast seaside resort – miles of clean sands with safe bathing, a pier, fine parks and gardens, an extensive shopping centre, numerous hotels and restaurants, entertainment facilities of every type. The **Russell-Cotes Museum** on the East Cliff is virtually a shrine to Victoriana. Near the pier, the modern **Oceanarium** displays many types of marine and freshwater life from around the world, and includes a walk-through tunnel within the shark tank!

It is somewhat incredible to think that, until 1812, there was nothing here except heath-covered cliffs and wooded chines (ravines) frequented by smugglers. In that year Lewis Tregonwell, who had previously patrolled the area as a Captain of Dragoons, built a summer residence. Finding that friends wished to lease the house, he built other holiday cottages nearby – this was the beginning of the resort of Bournemouth. Tregonwell's original house is now part of the Exeter Hotel, and his name is commemorated in one of the halls of the **Bournemouth International Centre** (the 'BIC').

Bournemouth

A337 to Cadnam, then A31 westbound and A338, follow brown signs for beaches. The A35 route via Christchurch is more direct, but passes through more built-up areas. 27 miles (43km) via Cadnam.
Bournemouth TIC:
☎ 08450 511 700

Christchurch

The original Saxon name of Christchurch was Twynham, meaning 'place between the waters', as the centre of the town lies between the Rivers Avon and Stour. The eleventh-century **Priory**, with its tall fifteenth-century tower, rates as the longest parish church in England at 312ft (95m), having been taken over by the town after the Dissolution.

The ruins of the **Norman Castle** and of the **Constable's House** are nearby, along with a variety of shops, tearooms, pubs and restaurants, while the **Red House Museum** is well worth a visit. The **Town Quay** area is picturesque and there are pleasant riverside walks. One of these leads over the marshes to **Hengistbury Head** (also accessible from the large car park at Southbourne). The headland has much biological and archaeological interest and provides superb views of the Isle of Wight and of Purbeck.

Highcliffe, now part of Christchurch, is separated from Barton-on-Sea by a chine with the delightful name of Chewton Bunny. **Highcliffe Castle**, built in the 1830s, was gutted by a disastrous fire in 1967. However, much of the exterior has been restored, as an example of 'the Romantic and Picturesque style of architecture'. A few rooms house an exhibition on the

---

Christchurch

A35 goes directly Lyndhurst-Christchurch. 16 miles (25.5km).
Christchurch TIC:
☎ 01202 471780.

history of the castle and special exhibitions through the season. The car park also gives access to **Highcliffe beach** and rapidly fills up in good weather.

Poole Quay and Brownsea Island

At **Tower Park**, Poole claims to have the 'largest entertainment centre in the south', with multi-screen cinema, ten-pin bowling, indoor water park and so on. The Dolphin shopping complex is also one of the largest in the region. However, for most visitors interest centres around bustling **Poole Quay**.

The **Waterfront Museum** contains a replica Victorian street and many other displays of life in and around Poole over the centuries. Pick up a leaflet on the Cockle Trail and follow the 82 brass plaques that guide you through over 750 years of Poole's history.

Poole Pottery has long been situated on The Quay, though the factory is no longer found here. Visitors may see the master potter working at his wheel and designers working in the Studio, before making purchases in the shop.

Ferries leave the quay for **Brownsea Island**, a peaceful place with nature trails through the woods, the site of Baden-Powell's first-ever Boy Scout camp and a nature reserve managed by the Dorset Wildlife Trust. It is one of the few remaining strongholds of the red squirrel in England.

Poole has its own seaside on the narrow peninsula of **Sandbanks**, from which a car ferry runs across the mouth of Poole Harbour to Shell Bay, giving access to Swanage, Corfe Castle and the beauties of the Isle of Purbeck.

Poole

As for Bournemouth, but stay on the A338 till it connects with the A35, follow signs to Poole Quay. 34 miles (54.5km).
Poole Welcome Centre:
☎ 01202 253253.

Wimborne Minster

The whole town takes its name from the **Minster church**, which dates mainly from the twelfth to fifteenth centuries. The building has an unusual 'mottled' appearance, being constructed from two types of stone, one grey and one a rich brown. On one of the two towers is the Quarter Jack, a figure dressed as a British grenadier of Napoleonic times, which strikes bells at every quarter hour. Inside the church is a remarkable Chained Library of 250 books, hardly altered since 1686.

In the streets around the Minster there are many fine Georgian town houses. The East Dorset Heritage Centre occupies the old **Market House** in the Cornmarket, now pedestrianised. **Wimborne Market**, however, has moved out of the town centre to a huge 4-acre (1.6-hectare) site, much of it under cover, and operates on Fridays, Saturdays and Sundays.

Wimborne Minster

A337 to Cadnam, then A31, 25 miles (40km)
Wimborne Minster TIC:
☎ 01202 886116.

Getting there

By rail

The main-line from London Waterloo to Weymouth passes through the Forest. The main Forest station is Brockenhurst, with other stations at Ashurst, (2½ miles (4km) from Lyndhurst), Beaulieu Road, Sway and New Milton. There are also direct services to Brockenhurst from the Midlands, the North and Scotland. Cycle hire is available very near Brockenhurst station – see 'Cycling' below. A branch line connects Brockenhurst with Lymington Town and Lymington Pier stations.

National Rail Enquiries: ☎ 0845 7484950 or www.thetrainline.com

By coach

National Express runs regular services stopping at Ringwood; Lyndhurst, Brockenhurst and Lymington are served less frequently. There is a full service to and from Southampton. National information and booking service
☎ 08705 808080
www.nationalexpress.co.uk

By car

Junction 1 of the M27 at Cadnam is 4 miles (6.4km) by the A337 from Lyndhurst. Beyond Cadnam, the M27 becomes the A31, passing through the Forest with few exit points before Ringwood. The M27 is reached from London by the M3; from Oxford, the Midlands and the North by the A34 and the M3; from Eastbourne and the South-east by the A27; and from Wales and Bristol by the A36. The A35 connects Honiton and the South-west directly with Lyndhurst.

By air

Bournemouth International Airport is 6 miles (9.5 km) from Bournemouth Central Station. Southampton International Airport is immediately adjacent to Southampton Parkway Station. Both stations are on the rail line which connects with the New Forest stations mentioned above.

By sea

Brittany Ferries from Cherbourg, Caen and St Malo to Portsmouth; and from Cherbourg to Poole ☎ 0870 5360360.

Condor Ferries from the Channel Islands and Brittany to Weymouth
☎ 01305 761551

LD Ferries from Le Havre to Portsmouth ☎ 0870 4580401.

Accommodation

Ample accommodation of all types is available in the New Forest and the surrounding area. *'The New Forest Where to Stay Guide'* includes approximately 60 hotels, guest houses and inns in every price range, obtainable for the Visitor Information Centres listed on p.109. In addition, there are over 180 bed and breakfast establishments, including farmhouses; and more than 70 listings for self-catering. There is a **Youth Hostel** at Cottesmore House, Cott Lane, Burley ☎ 01425 403233.

Camping and caravanning

The **Forestry Commission** runs ten camping and caravan sites deep in the heart of the Forest ☎ 0131 314 6505. They range from the 700 pitches at Holmsley, with all facilities including power points for caravans, to Matley Wood with 70 pitches and minimal facilities (bring your own toilet tent!). The *'Where to Stay Guide'* also lists several commercial sites of which only **Red Shoot Camping Park** near Ringwood (☎ 01425 473789) is within the perambulation.

Holiday Parks

Sandy Balls Country Holidays (☎ 01435 653067) near Fordingbridge has won a David Bellamy Gold Conservation Award. It has also been given an 'England for Excellence' Award – as have the following, nearer the coast in the New Milton area: **Hoburne Bashley** (☎ 01425 612340) and **Shorefield Country Park** (☎ 01590 648331).

Self-catering cottages (Agencies)

New Forest Cottages
☎ 01590 679655

Bournemouth Holiday Homes
☎ 01258 858580

Hideaways
☎ 01747 828170

The New Forest Breakfast

Why not ask if your accommodation offers the New forset Breakfast? The taste is great and ingredients are sourced locally, reducing food miles, supporting farmers and other producers in the Forest and helping the local economy. If self-catering, ingredients may be brought at these outlets:

Sunnyfields Organics
nr Totton
☎ 023 8087 1408

Owls Barn Organic Farm
nr Christchurch
☎ 01425 672239

Charford Farm Foods
nr Fordingbridge
☎ 01725 510093

Hazel Copse Farm Shop
nr Beaulieu
☎ 01590 612696

www.newforestproduce.com

Annual Events

Consult the Events leaflet from the VICs or the New Forest web-site. Events usually include:

Fordingbridge Show
Saturday in mid-July

Bucklers Hard Village Festival
Saturday in mid-July

New Forest and Hampshire County Show
New Park, Brockenhurst, 3 days in late July

Netley Marsh Steam Engine Rally
nr Totton, weekend in late July

Romsey Show
Second Saturday in September

Carnivals
Romsey (late July)
Lymington (mid-August)
Brockenhurst (late August)
Ringwood (late September).

Breamore House, the **Beaulieu complex, Exbury** and **Broadlands** at Romsey each hold a number of special events throughout the season.

Paultons Park and Marwell Wildlife
Become 'Christmas Wonderlands' each December.

Cycling

Cycling is an excellent way to get to know the New Forest, covering more ground than on foot, while penetrating deep into the woodlands.

At least nine organisations in the area hire out adults' and children's bikes and tandems. Most also offer tagalongs (adult/child 'tandems'), child seats, bratmobiles (towed cabins for under-fives) and even mutmobiles for dogs or cargo! Accessories, helmets and route maps are generally included without extra charge. There are also several publications available showing routes in and around the Forest.

Cyclists are permitted to use sensitively waymarked routes through the Forest. Over 100 miles (160km) of gravel tracks link the main centres by the safest and most scenic routes.

AA Bike Hire
Gosport Lane, Lyndhurst
☎ 023 8028 3349

Ashley Cycles
Ashley Road, New Milton
☎ 01425 618103

Balmer Lawn Bike Hire
Balmer Lawn Road, Brockenhurst
☎ 01590 623133

Brockenhurst Cycle Experience
The Island Shop, Brockenhurst
☎ 01590 624204

Forest Leisure Cycling
Village Centre, Burley
☎ 01425 403584

Country Lanes Cycle Centre
Brockenhurst Railway Station – also supported group tours and self-guided itineraries
☎ 01590 622627

Forest Leisure Cycling
Village Centre, Burley
☎ 01425 403584

Rentabike/On Yer Bike Tours
Manchester Road, Sway
☎ 01590 681876

Sandy Balls Cycle Centre
Godshill, Fordingbridge
☎ 01425 657707

Facilities for the disabled

Entries in this guide include facilities for the disabled where known. Bolderwood, Blackwater, Wilverley Plain and Hatchet Pond Forest car parks provide disabled toilet facilities. Three waymarked walks from Bolderwood, two from Blackwater and one from Wilverley are suitable for wheelchairs, although some include hills.

The Visitor Information Centres issue a four-page leaflet *Attractions with Facilities for the Disabled Visitor*, which covers the Forest and a quite wide area around it.

Ferries and cruises

Puffin Cruises
Town Quay, Lymington. Isle of Wight passenger service, cruises in Lymington River and the Solent. Trips to Needles & Lighthouse available.
☎ 07850 947618
www.puffincruiseslymington.com

Bucklers Hard Maritime Museum
Bookings taken for short cruises on the Beaulieu River.
☎ 01590 616203
www.bucklershard.co.uk

White Horse Ferries (Hythe Ferry)
Frequent passenger ferry service from Hythe Pier to Town Quay Southampton.
☎ 023 8084 0722
www.hytheferry.co.uk

Keyhaven Ferry

Passenger services to Hurst Castle and to the Isle of Wight, Solent cruises.
☎ 01590 642500

Wightlink

Ferry Terminal, Lymington. Half-hourly car and passenger service to Yarmouth, Isle of Wight.
☎ 0871 376 1000
www.wightlink.co.uk

Isle of Wight tourist information

☎ 01983 813813

Fishing

Permits are available for coarse fishing in **Hatchet Pond** and **Cadman's Pool**, obtainable from Forestry Commission offices and camp-sites or from shops in the area (including Leisure Fayre, Lyndhurst). **Janesmoor Pond** may be used without charge by (accompanied) junior anglers only; while Roundhill Pond may be used by juniors staying at Roundhill camp-site. Fishing is not permitted in New Forest streams or in any of the 300 or so other ponds. An Environment Agency rod licence must be purchased by anyone wishing to fish in any water in England.

These are commercial fisheries (coarse unless otherwise stated) in or near the Forest:

Avon Tyrell House

Near Ringwood ☎ 01425 672347

Beeches Brook Fishery

Burley ☎ 01425 402373

Broadlands Lake

Romsey ☎ 023 8086 9881

Broadlands Estate

(Disabled facilities) ☎ 023 8073 9438 (also trout fishing)

Everton Grange Lake

Milford-on-Sea ☎ 01590 642008

Holbury Trout Lakes

Lockerley, near Romsey
☎ 01794 341610

Hordle Lakes

Golden Hill, Hordle
☎ 01590 672300

Lake Farm Fishery

Sandleheath, Fordingbridge
☎ 01425 653383

Mopley Farm Cadland Fishery

Blackfield, near Fawley
☎ 023 8089 1617

Orchard Lakes

Near New Milton ☎ 01425 612404

Rockbourne Trout Fishery

Near Fordingbridge
☎ 01425 518603

Sway lakes

Barrows Lane, Sway
☎ 01590 682010

Turfcroft Farm Fishery

Burley (disabled facilities)
☎ 01425 403743

Glossary – New Forest words

The special nature of the New Forest extends to the use of unusual words and unusual meanings for common words. This is a selection.

A & O
Ancient and Ornamental Woodland; unfenced woods grazed by domestic stock

Agister
Official employed by the Verderers, responsible for the welfare of the commoners' animals

Bottom
(In place-names) a valley in heathland

Cob
Traditional building material of clay and straw

Commoner
Person using the common rights which attach to the property where he or she lives

Depastured
(Of stock) living on the open Forest

Drift
An autumn round-up of ponies in an area of the Forest

Driftway
A broad 'corridor' of open land between two inclosures, providing a link for stock between grazing areas

Estovers
(Common right of) entitlement to 'fuelwood' from the Forest

Expeditation
Ancient practice of removing toes from large dogs to prevent them hunting deer; also known as 'lawing'

Fence month
Two weeks on each side of midsummer, when most young deer are born; formerly all domestic stock had to be removed from the forest

Fern
Local name for bracken

Furze
Local name for gorse

Gutter
(In place-names) a stream

Hat
(In place-names) a small copse on heathland, often roughly circular and containing many holly bushes

Heyning
Winter period when grazing is poor; formerly all domestic stock had to be removed from the Forest

Inclosure
(Yes, this is the correct spelling!) a fenced woodland, where stock cannot enter, originally for commercial timber production, now also managed for conservation and amenity.

Lawn
An area of closely cropped grassland; the best grazing in the Forest

Marl
(Common right of) the right to dig clay as fertiliser or building material; no longer practised

Mast
(Common right of) the right to release pigs to feed in the open forest

Pannage
The period of the year when the right of mast can be practised

Passage
A causeway through a bog

Perambulation
The traditional boundary of the Forest, last extended in 1964

Pollarded
Applied to a tree which had branches cut when it was young, resulting in several main branches rather than one trunk

Presentment
A verbal application or statement made to the Verderers during their open court

Purlieu
An area on the forest edge, historically freed from Forest Law

Ride
A wide trackway through woodland

Shade
An established spot where ponies and cattle regularly gather in hot weather (also used as a verb)

Turbary
(Common right of) the right to cut turf (peat) for fuel; no longer practised

Verderers
The ten officials who meet in open court ten times a year and whose major function is to protect the rights of the commoners

Water
(In place-names) a stream

Golf

Barton-on-Sea Golf Club
☎ 01425 615308

Bramshaw Golf Club
☎ 023 8081 3433

Brockenhurst Manor Golf Club
☎ 01590 623332

Burley Golf Club
(9 holes)
☎ 01425 402431

Dibden Golf Centre
near Hythe
☎ 023 8084 5596

Hamptworth Golf and Country Club
☎ 01794 390155

New Forest Golf Club
Lyndhurst
☎ 023 8028 2752

Paultons Golf Centre
☎ 023 8081 3345

Walhampton Golf Course
nr. Lymington
☎ 01590 689631

Guided walks

The Forestry Commission publishes an annual *'What's On'* leaflet which lists a variety of walks and activities within the Forest run by the Rangers, from April till Christmas. These run at various times of day, and have previously included deer-watching, the dawn chorus, and 'creatures of the twilight'. There may be opportunities to visit a commercial woodland with a forester, to learn from the skills of a wildlife artist or to join a storyteller in the depths of the woods. There are small charges for most of these events, but even the free ones need to be pre-booked.

Information and booking ☎ 023 8028 3141.

There are regular Guided Walks, led by professional guides registered with the Institute of Tourist Guiding, in each of the towns and cities listed in the 'Excursions' chapter. These are highly recommended; details may be obtained from TICs.

Horse riding

All the following establishments offer direct access to the Forest, for rides from one hour upwards, for both beginners and experienced riders.

Arniss Riding Stables
Godshill, near Fordingbridge
☎ 01425 654114

Bagnum Riding Centre
Near Ringwood
☎ 01425 476263

Burley Manor Riding Stables
☎ 01425 403489

Burley-Villa School of Riding
Bashley near New Milton; 'Western Riding in the New Forest'
☎ 01425 610278

Fir Tree Farm Equestrian Centre
Ogdens, near Fordingbridge
☎ 01425 654744

Ford Farm Stables
Burley Road, Brockenhurst
☎ 01590 623043

Forest Park Riding Centre
Rhinefield Road, Brockenhurst
☎ 01590 623429

Silver Horseshoe Riding Centre
Hale, near Fordingbridge
☎ 01725 510678

Sims Cottage Stables
Wilverley Road, New Milton
☎ 01425 612961

Warborne Farm Stables
Pilley, Near Lymington
☎ 01590 673999

Maps

The whole of the New Forest is covered by Ordnance Survey Explorer map OL22 (New Forest) at a scale of 2½ inches to 1 mile (4cm to 1km) and this map is **very highly recommended** to all visitors.

In the OS Landranger (1¼ inch to 1 mile or 2cm to 1km) series, the Forest is divided between sheets 195 (Bournemouth) and 196 (Solent and Isle of Wight).

Markets

Christchurch – Monday
Highcliffe – Friday
Hythe – Tuesday
Lymington – Saturday
Ringwood – Wednesday
Romsey – Tuesday and Friday
Salisbury – Tuesday and Saturday
Totton – Wednesday
Wimborne – Friday, Saturday, Sunday
Winchester – Wednesday, Friday and Saturday

Farmer's Markets – second and last Sundays of the month in Winchester (except end of December); also occasional Sundays at Romsey, Ringwood, Hythe, Beaulieu, Lyndhurst and Lymington. ☎ 023 8028 5428

Parking

Parking in the main centres such as Lyndhurst, Brockenhurst, Fordingbridge, Ringwood and Lymington is provided by New Forest District Council on a Pay-and-Display system. However, visitors might save money by purchasing an annual parking time-clock, valid in all NFDC car-parks.

The car parks sited within the open forest are provided by the Forestry Commission. The most popular ones have toilet facilities – Blackwater, Whitefield Moor, Wilverley Plain, Hatchet Pond, Reptile Centre. Anderwood and Wilverley Inclosures have **barbecue sites** (bookable ☎ 023 8028 3141). Other popular spots include Knightwood, Rufus Stone, Bolton's Bench and Balmer Lawn. There are around 110 other small car parks within the Forest – but a number have been closed recently to protect sensitive environments; they will still be found on older maps. Some car parks have advisory Pay-and-Display meters; money contributed benefits the general management of the New Forest.

Public transport

The New Forest suffers from too many cars. Using public transport will help to reduce pollution and congestion – and enable visitors to undertake linear walks. A very frequent train service crosses the Forest and there are reasonably frequent bus services between Southampton, Lyndhurst, Brockenhurst and Lymington, as well as along the Waterside and the Avon Valley. Other villages are less frequently served, but careful use of the 'New Forest Annual Travel Guide' will make most journeys possible. www.thenewforestfour.info

Swimming pools & leisure centres

New Forest Leisure Information booking line: ☎ 0845 659 0845

Seawater Baths (Open-air)
Bath Road, Lymington
☎ 01590 674865

The Rapids of Romsey
☎ 01794 830333

Applemore Recreation Centre
Dibden, near Hythe

Calshot Activity Centre
Calshot Spit

Lymington Recreation Centre
North Street, Pennington

New Milton Recreation Centre
Gore Road, New Milton

Ringwood Recreation Centre
Parsonage Barn Lane, Ringwood

Totton Recreation Centre
Water Lane, Totton

Visitor Information Centres

Lymington Visitor Information Centre
New Street, Lymington, SO41 9BH
☎ 01590 689000
Fax 01590 689090

Lyndhurst Visitor Information Centre
☎ 023 8029 2269
www.thenewforest.co.uk
e-mail: information@nfdc.gov.uk

Ringwood
☎ 01425 470896
www.thenewforest.co.uk

Fordingbridge
☎ 01425 654560
Open Mon–Sat 10am–4pm
Only open in the summer season.

See also boxes in the 'Excursions' chapter.

Weather

Seven-day forecasts for Hampshire, Weathercall ☎ 09068 500 403 (premium rate).
BBC local weather online: www.bbc.co.uk/hampshire/weather/forecast

*A cord of timber ready
for collection*

*A pollarded
beech tree*

Index

Published by
Landmark Publishing Ltd,
The Oaks, Moor Farm Road West, Ashbourne, Derbyshire, DE6 1HD
Tel: (01335) 347349 Fax: (01335) 347303
www.landmark publishing.co.uk

ISBN: 978-1-84306-454-1

© **Gerald Ponting 2009**
4th Edition

Print: Gutenberg Press Ltd, Malta
Design & Cartography: Michelle Prost

Front cover: New Forest mare and foal on Swan Green, Lyndhurst
Back cover top: Palace House
Back Cover Middle: Autumn colours, New Forest
Back Cover Bottom: Fallow Deer
Back Cover Right: Shafts of sunlight on a spring morning create a magical effect among the pine trees of King's Hat Inclosure

Picture Credits

Any photography not credited below is by the author.

Beaulieu Enterprises Ltd: Back Cover Top, 62, 63 bottom, 66, 67 middle
Breamore House (www.breamorehouse.com): 43, 47 top, 50 top
Brian J Woodruffe: 15 middle, 78 top
Exbury Gardens Ltd:63 top, 74 both
International Photobank (www.internationalphotobank.co.uk): Back Cover Middle
Marwell Wildlife: 91 top, 95 bottom right
New Forest Cider: 51, 58 top
New Forest District Council (www.thenewforest.com): 6, 7, 19, 23 top, 23 bottom left, 30
New Forest & Hampshire County Show: 31 all
New Forest National Park Authority/CMJ Matthews (www.newforestnpa.gov.uk): Back cover bottom, 59 top
New Forest National Park Authority/Martin O'Neill (www.newforestnpa.gov.uk): 34 top, 22 top, 10 top
New Forest National Park Authority/Paul Close (www.newforestnpa.gov.uk): 22 bottom
Paultons Park (www.paultonspark.co.uk): 90, 95 top
Phil Green: 2 bottom left. 10 middle left, 11 bottom, 11 bottom left
St Barbe Museum, Lymington: 83 both
Spinners Garden: 87 bottom
The Verderers of the New Forest: 38
The New Forest Otter, Owl & Wildlife Conservation Park, Nicole Duplaix: 70 both
Winchester City Council (www.visitwinchester.co.uk): 95 bottom left
www.historicdockyard.co.uk: 98 all

The following images are courtesy of www.shutterstock.com with copyright to:
Susannah Grant: 99 top; David Peta: 27 bottom, 34 middle;
Leslie Budzynski: 99 bottom right; Shoarns: 32; Richard Melichar: 94